Letting Go…

A Mother's Journey

Lenora Reneé Scurry

The moral right of the author has been asserted.

Text Copyright © 2024 by **Lenora Scurry**

All rights reserved. No part of this book may be reproduced, stored in a retrieval system, or transmitted in any form or by any means, electronic, mechanical, photocopying, recording, public performances or otherwise, without written permission of **Lenora Scurry**, except for brief quotations embodied in critical articles or reviews. The book is for personal and commercial use by the Author, **Lenora Scurry.**

The right of **Lenora Scurry** to be identified as the author of this work has been asserted in accordance with sections 77 and 78 of the copyright Designs and Patents Act 1988.

Book Cover Design: Lisa Line

Editing: Nick Cappello

Typesetting / Proofreading: Nick Cappello

Publishing: Lenora Scurry, LLC.

Copyright © 2024 Lenora Reneė Scurry

All rights reserved.

ISBN: 979-8-9901103-1-1

DISCLAIMER

This memoir's contents represent the author's personal opinions, reflections, and experiences. These views are entirely their own and do not necessarily reflect those of any other individual, organization, or entity.

This memoir is written solely to share personal stories and perspectives. It is not intended to create conflict, harm, or offense to any individual or group.

Readers are encouraged to approach the text with an open mind and an understanding that it is a subjective account shaped by the author's unique experiences and viewpoints.

DEDICATION

To my sweet baby girl, Kerry, and my precious grandbabies, I dedicate this book to you with all my love.

Kerry, I'm so sorry I wasn't the mother you needed. I have so many regrets. I just know that if I could do it over, I would do things so differently. I know this book is going to hurt you, but we have to break this cycle so we can heal, and the only way to do that is to stop burying our secrets.

My prayer is that you find your way to all the love and happiness you deserve! I know your actions are from trauma, just as mine were. I gave you everything that my pain didn't take. I will always be here for you when you're ready; I love you to the moon and back!

To my cherished grandbabies, you have been such a joy in my life, and I hope you have enough precious memories to never forget me. There is never a day goes by that I don't think of you, and my heart aches to have you in my life again. Always remember your life is what you make it by your choices. Spread your wings and fly.

"You are my sunshine, my only sunshine."

I love you up to Jesus and back down again!

GRANDMA AND GRANDDAD, MY BIGGEST SUPPORTERS

INTRODUCTION

Why do I want to write this book?

What do I hope to achieve?

These questions were uppermost in my mind when I embarked on this project, and neither were easy to answer.

"Why" is perhaps the simplest of the two - there was a deep need in me to understand the events that led to the situation I find myself in. So much has happened, and digging into the past, recalling situations, reliving the emotions in an attempt to somehow make sense of everything has actually been very cathartic for me. I would liken it to a snake shedding its skin - only multiple times and in a short period.

As for what I hope to achieve…if one person reads this book, recognizes the signs I perhaps missed in my family and is able to course correct to prevent something similar from happening to them - well then, I will feel that the pain I have undergone was in some way worth it.

Letting Go… A Mother's Journey

MOM AND DAD, WHERE IT ALL BEGAN

TABLE OF CONTENTS

DISCLAIMER III
DEDICATION IV
WHY DO I WANT TO WRITE THIS BOOK? VI
TABLE OF CONTENTS VIII
CHAPTER 1 WHERE IT ALL STARTED - MY EARLY CHILDHOOD 1
CHAPTER 2 NEEDING TO BE WANTED 10
CHAPTER 3 TIME TO LEAVE 24
CHAPTER 4 MY HERO 33
CHAPTER 5 ECHOES OF LOVE AND BETRAYAL 40
CHAPTER 6 THE DARKNESS RETURNS 53
CHAPTER 7 MISTAKES MADE WITH GOOD INTENTIONS 66
CHAPTER 8 THERE'S ALWAYS LIGHT AT THE END OF THE TUNNEL 73
CHAPTER 9 SETTING BOUNDARIES 80
CHAPTER 10 THE OUTSIDER 91
CHAPTER 11 PUTTING THE KIDS FIRST ALWAYS 98
CHAPTER 12 OPENING PANDORA'S BOX 108
CHAPTER 13 THE TRUTH CAN HURT – LEARNING TO LET GO 119
CHAPTER 14 LEAVING LOVE'S DOOR AJAR 130
EPILOGUE 137
APPENDIX 142
ABOUT THE AUTHOR 151

CHAPTER 1

WHERE IT ALL STARTED - MY EARLY CHILDHOOD

Don't tell me who to be. I'll tell you who I am.
-Lenora Scurry-

As I write this book, the weather lately has been almost the same as it was in Berea, Kentucky, back in 1961, when my story began. The memories contained within this book rise like ghosts, some sharp and clear as crystal, others blurred by time and trauma. But to understand how I got here—how my daughter and I ended up where we are now—I need to go all the way back to the beginning.

I was born on an incredibly hot April day in Madison County, though we actually lived in Lexington, about 40 minutes away. My mother had been visiting her mother when her labor began, a seemingly innocent circumstance that somehow feels symbolic of the chaos that would define my early years. I came into this world as the youngest of six children, with age gaps that felt like canyons for the most part: Sheri (born 1948), Jim (1951), Rob (1953), Melissa (1956), and Tony (1959). Tony and I were only 18 months apart, though. Even decades later, I wonder if I was an unplanned, unwanted final addition to an already full house. Sheri became more of a stand-in mom rather than a sister on occasion, and she, Jim, and Rob (who were the closest things to friends and parents that I had) left the family home as I reached my teenage years.

My parents divorced when I was just a year old, so my siblings and I would visit with my father every other weekend. The rest of the time, we lived with my mother in an old country-style plantation house. It wasn't grand and desperately needed renovation, but it was home. As a single parent, Mom had to work multiple jobs to earn the money to care for the six of us, yet she still found time to make all our clothes and put delicious home-cooked food on the table.

Looking back from an adult perspective, I wonder how she managed. She must have been exhausted all the time, with little left to offer in the way of loving attention to her brood of children. In the same breath, I wonder why she appeared to single me out for negative attention. I don't recall her ever praising me, saying I looked pretty, or even just sitting and talking to me.

What I do recall vividly is the way she would seek to ridicule or put me down, and as I said earlier, I wonder if that is because she hadn't wanted another child. I remember one occasion clearly; I must have been around four. My mother had taken a photograph of me. Once the photos returned, she looked at them, turned to me, and said, "This would have been a great picture if only you weren't so fat."

ACTUAL PHOTO FROM THAT DAY

At four years old, I couldn't understand why my mother would say something so horrible to me. All I knew was that her words made me feel unloved, unwanted, and bad about myself. No child should have to make sense of why their mommy doesn't love them. Those words evoked feelings too big, too heavy for my small heart to carry.

I think it must also have been around this time that my mom began to punish me with regard to food. Cupboards containing food were locked. My other siblings were offered snacks and treats while I was not, and I was constantly reminded, often in front of my brothers and sisters, that I was fat.

It was a dark time for a little girl. A little girl who was both sensitive and intelligent, and I am 100% positive my lifelong battle with weight began during this period. Left to enjoy food like any other kid, I'm pretty sure the baby fat of childhood would have naturally melted away. Little did I know it was the beginning of my constant struggle with making a puzzle piece fit. Like all children, I believed the pieces I was given were the right ones – that if I just turned them enough times or pressed hard enough, they would finally click into place.

As it was, food was always an issue in the house, and rather than lose weight as my mother constantly bullied me to do, I turned to a negative cycle of binge eating when I was about nine years old—eating until I became sick to the point of vomiting. It became my guilty pleasure, and boy, did I feel guilty! But the binging was the one thing I, as a little girl, could control myself. Mom could try to dictate what I ate, what I did, how I dressed, but for brief moments of time, I could take back some self-determination and gorge myself to the point of sickness, then hide in my room underneath the yellow candlewick comforter until my tummy calmed down.

Food wasn't the only thing controlled in that household; the religion my mother practiced, The United Pentecostal Church, shunned the watching of TV, and we weren't allowed to have one in the house. However, my father wanted us children to have one and, therefore, installed an old half-working television in the musty dirt cellar underneath the house. The setup was completed by a raggedy old brown couch and chair, and my brother Tony and I would sit in that dark, dank cellar and watch kids' TV shows.

Looking back now, the absurdity of that basement TV strikes me as a perfect metaphor for the contradictions that ruled our childhood. It was as if relegating the television to that underground space somehow made it less sinful, less worldly – as though God's disapproving gaze couldn't penetrate the foundation of our house. We were allowed to consume this "forbidden fruit" only in the shadows, like guilty thieves, while our home maintained its pretense of pious perfection upstairs. In my adult years, I've often wondered if this wasn't my first lesson in religious hypocrisy – the peculiar human talent for bending the rules without technically breaking them. With its fuzzy reception and perpetual air of secrecy, that basement TV taught me more about adult double standards than any sermon ever could.

But I digress; the TV was square in the old style, with a beige plastic covering and rusty metal legs. It was plugged into a power socket suspended from the ceiling. Sometimes, the TV would turn on just fine, and on other occasions, it wouldn't. My brother Tony and I had a little routine for when the TV wouldn't come straight on.

Letting Go... A Mother's Journey

REPRESENTATION OF THE TV THAT ALMOST KILLED ME

Being older by 18 months, Tony, the big brother, climbed that rickety ladder to mess with the socket while I'd lay flat on my back under the TV set. I remember clear as day how those cold metal legs felt against my hands, my eyes squinting up at all the dust and wires hanging down. We had it down to a science: Tony would plug the tv in while I watched for the little red light that meant freedom was coming. Half-hour wait time, that's what we knew to expect – just enough time to play some made-up games to pass the minutes till cartoon time.

We must've gone through that same routine a hundred times over, just two kids trying to squeeze some fun out of that basement. We didn't know any better – couldn't see how close we were playing with danger. Then came that one day, me being six years old when our little TV-fixing game almost turned into something that would change everything. Looking back now, I think that was the first real sign that things in our family weren't just bent; they were fixing to break clean through.

There I was, like always, gripping those rusted metal legs of the TV while Tony climbed up to fiddle with the plug. The cellar's familiar mustiness hung around me, dirt floor cold against my back, just another ordinary afternoon – until it wasn't. That's when it hit me – electricity surging through my small body with a force I couldn't comprehend, turning my muscles to stone. Each second stretched into an eternity as the current buzzed through me, my hands welded to the metal like they'd become part of the TV stand itself. Strange how I can't remember if it hurt – they told me later the shock scrambled my memories – but I'll never forget trying to scream for Tony and finding my voice had vanished. Just silence while that current held me captive against the dirt floor, my body betraying me in ways I didn't understand.

Above me, Tony kept asking if I had seen that red light yet, his voice echoing off the cellar walls like nothing was wrong. I could hear him clear as day, could even see his feet shifting impatiently on the ladder rungs, but my voice was trapped somewhere inside me, buried under waves of electricity. He got frustrated and told me, "If you're gonna act like that, I'm going upstairs." I was screaming his name in my mind over and over, begging him to look down, to see something wasn't right, but my mouth wouldn't obey. I watched helplessly as his feet disappeared, in my mind's eye, following his familiar path up past the little hill beside the house, climbing those porch steps through the big white door into the front room. I lay there listening to the family moving around upstairs – footsteps creaking across floorboards, voices drifting down, the sounds of normal life continuing while I remained pinned to the earth below them, feeling like I was buried alive with electricity coursing through me, unable to break free.

Letting Go... A Mother's Journey

CHILDHOOD HOME IN VERSAILLES, KY WHERE I WAS ELECTROCUTED

I don't know how long I stayed frozen like that – minutes or hours; time lost all meaning when every second was a battle to move, to speak, to break free from the current's grip. But Tony, knowing how I hated being alone in that cellar, finally came back down to check on me. Maybe he heard something in the silence, sensed something in my absence, or just felt a flicker of brotherly duty. Looking back now, I realize that was the one and only time in all my years I can remember my brother showing any real concern for what happened to me. It would take nearly dying on that dirt floor to glimpse a moment of genuine care from my own blood.

Tony stumbled back into that cellar, his footsteps slower now, uncertain. When he found me still frozen in place, exactly as he'd left me, something must have told him this wasn't just his little sister being difficult. He reached out and touched my arm – and the shock threw him backward like he'd been hit by a truck. The look on his face changed from an annoyed big brother to a terrified kid in an instant as he bolted back up toward the house, screaming to get help.

That's when everything shifted. I felt myself lifting away from my body, floating up toward the cellar ceiling like a forgotten balloon. Below me, I could see myself still trembling on that dirt floor, hands locked around those metal legs like they were welded there. I watched, detached and peaceful, as Mom and my oldest brother burst into the cellar. Their faces told a story my floating self couldn't quite feel – pure horror as they realized they couldn't pry my hands free, couldn't risk climbing that ladder to pull the plug. Through it all, my body kept shaking, electricity dancing through it like some kind of cruel puppet master.

From my perch near the ceiling, I saw my eldest brother's desperate solution – grabbing a piece of lumber, a thick two-by-four, and swinging it with everything he had, hoping to break the circuit between my hands and that sinful TV. The crack of wood against metal was like thunder in that small space, and suddenly, I was being yanked back down, slammed into my body like I'd been dropped from the sky. Everything after that becomes a blur of fragments and darkness.

Did Mom gather me up then? Did she hold me close and whisper prayers into my hair? I want to believe she did – after all, I was her baby girl, her youngest, and there I was, slipping away right before her eyes. But that memory, if it exists, is lost to the shock that nearly claimed my life.

The next clear piece I have is chaos – police arriving before the ambulance, making split-second decisions that would determine whether I lived or died. They bundled me into their squad car; my small body limp like a rag doll, water pouring from my mouth like a broken faucet. I was beyond unresponsive – as I would later learn, I was technically dead. The hospital brought me back but with no promises. "She probably won't make it through the night," they told my mother, their words cutting through her like knives.

But that little girl – me – wasn't done fighting. I survived that first night, though the doctors kept their grave faces. They painted a future filled with wheelchairs and feeding tubes, warning about brain damage and permanent vegetative states. They listed all the things I might never do again: walk, talk, and live a normal life.

The time in the hospital is mostly a blank space in my memory now, and the days that followed are lost in a fog I can't quite penetrate. Maybe that's a blessing. What matters is that somehow, against every prediction and probability, I clawed my way back to being whole. Not only did I walk and talk again, but Mom loves to say that once I started talking, I made up for lost time and haven't stopped since. How's that for beating the odds?

Looking back now, with adult eyes and decades of perspective, I wonder if that early brush with death somehow set the tone for my life to come. Did surviving against those odds make me stronger, or did it leave both visible and invisible scars that would shape my future in ways I couldn't understand? Certainly, it didn't change my mother's overall attitude. If anything, her emotional distance and criticism intensified after my recovery, as if my continued existence was somehow an affront to her expectations.

CHAPTER 2

NEEDING TO BE WANTED

Learn to love yourself. Your life depends on it.
-Lenora Scurry-

The near-death experience in that dank, dark cellar did nothing to soften my mother's attitude toward me. It instead gave her license to mock my weight. By age eight, I had developed a complicated relationship with food that would haunt me for decades to come. The shame and secrecy of binge eating became my constant companions, and by ten, my rebellious nature erupted like a long-dormant volcano.

I started smoking cigarettes, a decision that led to one of the more bizarre punishments my mother devised. When she discovered my habit, she forced me to eat an entire pack of cigarettes. I can still taste the disgusting tobacco, feel it coating my tongue and throat as I gagged and retched. "That's your problem," she said coldly as I vomited, "and it's exactly what you deserve." But her "creative" punishment backfired spectacularly - it only made me more determined to keep smoking, if only to spite her.

The holidays were particularly excruciating. Thanksgiving, Christmas, and any family gathering became an exercise in humiliation. My mother would watch every morsel I put on my plate like a hawk, her commentary sharp and cutting: "Oh my God, it's no wonder you're so fat; look at all that food!" She'd announce this to the entire gathering, ensuring maximum embarrassment. Eventually, I learned to retreat to my room during these celebrations, finding solace in solitude rather than face her public ridicule.

Food became my first drug of choice, a salvation that would ultimately betray me. My hands would tremble as I reached for another bite, my heart pounding with a mixture of defiance and shame. When I think about it now, with decades of perspective and my own experience as a mother, I'm haunted by the twisted logic of it all. Each bite was an act of defiance and surrender, my throat tight with unshed tears.

"Do you really need that second helping?" my mother would sneer, her words piercing the armor I tried so desperately to maintain. The fork would freeze halfway to my mouth, my stomach clenching with familiar dread. "Everyone's looking at how much you're eating." I wanted to scream back at her, to defend myself, but the words would die in my throat, replaced by the mechanical motion of chewing, swallowing, surviving.

My mother's voice became the narrator of every meal, transforming our dinner table into a battlefield where I fought daily for scraps of dignity. "You're getting so fat," she'd say, her eyes narrowing with disgust that cut me to my core. "You're embarrassing me." Each word was another brick in the wall of self-hatred I was building around myself. In those quiet moments alone with my binges, I found a desperate kind of peace - the peace of a drowning person clutching at anything that floats. Food didn't judge me. Food didn't hate me. Food filled the aching void her cruelty left behind.

Once I got older and started participating in holidays again, her eyes would still bore into me, calculating each bite like an accountant tallying debts. "People are staring at you," she'd whisper, leaning in close enough that only I could hear, her breath hot against my ear. "Look at how much food you're putting on your plate." My hands would shake as I tried to make myself smaller and invisible while shame burned through me like acid. Even now, decades later, I can hear those words as clearly as if she were sitting next to me, still watching, still judging, still waiting to point out every flaw. The little girl inside me still flinches at the memory, still yearns for a mother's love that came without conditions, without criticism, without the constant weight of disapproval.

My mother's sole purpose seemed to be forcing me to be as skinny as she thought I should be so that I wouldn't embarrass her. Her next logical step was to take me to Weight Watchers. I didn't know it then, but Mom had her own demons around food. She had been on one kind of diet or another for as long as I could remember, and she was on friendly terms with ex-lax pills and various "miracle" potions designed to stop people from gaining weight. She would vomit after each meal, but back then, we didn't know anything about bulimia. It wasn't until years later, as I began to research my own food addiction that I realized that's what my mother was experiencing. I don't even think she knew this wasn't normal behavior because it was something she never tried to hide.

The memory of that first Weight Watchers meeting is seared into my brain. Mom was thrifty - she had to be - and she made all of our clothes. They were never in the latest styles, and the fabrics were rarely the color or pattern we kids would have picked. But she tried. On this particular occasion, she insisted I wear a particularly ugly outfit she had made for me. The fabric was covered in big red, white, and blue stripes and stars. There were puffy sleeves and a vest, and the ensemble was completed with black Mary Jane shoes and white ankle socks. I looked and felt like a clown walking into that meeting room.

I am often drawn back to those Weight Watchers meetings—an arena where my mother's words rang out like a judge's gavel, sealing my fate. As was customary, the leader prompted everyone to introduce themselves, and when it was our turn, my mother stood up with a practiced poise. She introduced herself with a bright smile, but her demeanor shifted dramatically when she turned to me. In that moment, she made me stand, exposing me in front of a group of strangers clad in an outfit I was already ashamed of, a tangible reminder of my perceived failures.

Her words cut deep as she described me as an embarrassment, a child whose sole purpose was to eat. "I don't know what to do with her anymore," she lamented, her voice dripping with frustration. I felt myself shrinking as if the very air around me conspired to make me smaller until I was no more than an inch tall. My heart pounded in my chest, a frantic drum echoing my panic. Heat rushed to my face, and I wished desperately for the ground to swallow me whole.

The familiar tide of rejection surged within me, a wave of feelings that often crashed over me but now felt amplified in front of those women I didn't know. How could my own mother stand there and wield her words like daggers? Why was I, her flesh and blood, so unworthy of love and acceptance? Why did it seem she harbored such disdain for me?

In the aftermath of that humiliating meeting, as I sought solace in the one thing that had always comforted me—food—I found myself spiraling deeper into a cycle of binge eating that only compounded my pain. It was a vicious cycle, one that food had never intended to perpetuate, but at that moment, it felt like my only refuge. Each morsel was a temporary balm, a fleeting comfort that would soon be overshadowed by the weight of my guilt and self-loathing.

I vividly remember one incident that stands out like a beacon of shame. My stepdad, at the time, worked for a company that sent him boxes of candy. He would sell them at full retail price, a small business venture that filled our home with temptation. The boxes were stashed beneath the bed he shared with my mother, a hidden treasure trove that called to me like a siren's song. One desperate afternoon, I decided to seize my chance.

With my heart racing, I slid into their room and dragged out a box, my hands trembling with excitement and fear. I tore it open and began to devour the candy bars inside, shoving them into my mouth one after another. I can still remember the name of the candy bar, Sidekick. That memory is etched in my mind forever. I scarcely chewed, hardly tasted; I was a ravenous creature, lost in a haze of sugar and shame. I didn't stop until the box was empty. But with each bar I consumed, the joy I sought quickly transformed into a suffocating cloud of misery. I knew, deep down, that my mother would find out, and her ridicule would be swift and merciless.

When the inevitable confrontation came, it was as if my worst fears had materialized. My mother discovered the empty box, and the fury in her eyes was palpable. That day, I felt the weight of her disappointment like a physical force. She took the belt to me, her voice a harsh barrage of insults—"fat slob," "nasty pig," "an embarrassment." Each word landed like a punch, further embedding the belief that I was unworthy of love and fundamentally flawed.

My stepdad, perhaps emboldened by my mother's cruelty, joined in the chorus of abuse. His verbal and emotional assaults felt like arrows, each one designed to wound. I remember once, so terrified of his looming presence, I jumped out of my bedroom window and ran to a neighbor's house, pleading for help. But in that time, intervening in another family's turmoil was seen as overstepping, and I was sent right back home, back to the very place I sought to escape.

To make matters worse, my brother Tony added to my torment. He was relentless—beating me, locking me in closets, hurling cruel insults that echoed my mother's disdain. "Fat pig," "slob," "lazy," he would sneer, his words a reflection of the chaos that surrounded us. "I hate you; I've always hated you." And my mother, rather than intervening, seemed to revel in his cruelty, almost encouraging it.

I can still recall a time when Tony blackened both my eyes. It was my father who noticed and, in a rare moment of concern, warned my mother that if he ever saw marks like that on me again, he would call the police. But that threat did little to change our reality. The beatings continued, and the names persisted—constant reminders that I was unwanted, unlovable, and undeserving of happiness.

During the darkest of days, as I endured the beatings and the ridicule, I often wondered how my worth could be so easily dismissed. It felt as though I was drowning in a sea of despair, the relentless waves of my mother's abuse and my family's cruelty threatening to pull me under. There was a painful irony in it all—I had not been born with these beliefs. I was not inherently flawed; I had simply become a product of the environment that surrounded me.

At around age twelve, I discovered roller skating. It was something I could excel at, and more importantly, it got me out of that oppressive house for long stretches. The rink offered "all-night sessions," so mom would drop me off at 7 PM and pick me up at 7 AM the next morning. Looking back now, I wonder what kind of mother would let her twelve-year-old daughter stay out all night, but at the time, I was just grateful for the escape.

REPRESENTATION OF THE RINK

The rink was a shabby place - the paint peeling from the walls, worn carpeting fraying at the edges, and that distinct smell of rental skates, floor wax, and concession stand food that every skating rink seemed to have. But it had a small café inside where we all could eat, hang out, and chat. It became my sanctuary. The moment I walked through those doors, the throbbing beat of the music and the swoosh of wheels on polished wood would wash over me. For those precious hours, whenever I glided around that rink, no one would judge me or make fun of me. I could just be myself.

But that freedom came with its own dangers. There were no attendance lists at the door - kids were just dropped off and left to their own devices. I would meet up with a girlfriend, and we'd hook up with groups of guys, usually older than us. Drugs and alcohol became a regular part of my nights, and I grew increasingly promiscuous, though not yet to the point of sex. Looking back now, I realize I was desperately searching for love and acceptance - just in all the wrong places.

One night, I met a guy who said he wanted to date me. Being twelve and starved for attention, I was thrilled when he came to introduce himself to my mother. He told her he was eighteen—a lie, as he was actually twenty-six. Now, as an adult and a mother myself, I wonder how any twenty-six-year-old man could want to date a twelve-year-old child. But Mom gave her blessing, and off we went.

The summer night air was thick and humid as we drove through the darkness to Jacobson Park in Lexington. My heart fluttered with excitement - finally, someone had chosen me, wanted me. The streetlights cast eerie shadows as we pulled into the deserted parking lot. The chirping of crickets and rustling leaves were the only sounds breaking the heavy silence.

When we got out of the car, I wasn't prepared for what came next. The park was pitch black except for distant lights that barely penetrated the darkness. My excitement turned to fear as his demeanor suddenly changed.

He raped me. He violated me. He made my soul as dark as that park on that particular night.

I was a twelve-year-old virgin, and he raped me. The pain was searing, terrifying. His weight crushed me as he held me down, the rough ground scraping against my back. I could smell beer on his breath and feel his stubble against my face as he forced himself on me. I was paralyzed with fear, unable to scream or fight back. The darkness seemed to close in around me as I retreated deep inside myself, trying to escape what was happening to my body.

What's sad is I didn't realize that's what it was until years later. Until then, I had always blamed myself. Everything else was my fault, so why not add this to the long list? I wasn't special to him at all; I was just an easy target. This was also the role I would find myself playing over and over again throughout my life.

When he'd finished, I noticed I was bleeding. In my naivety, I didn't understand what was happening to my body. I truly thought I was dying. Mom never talked to us about sex or boys; she didn't even prepare us for our periods. I couldn't call her - I knew she would blame me. I ended up calling a friend, and she and her momma came and picked me up. Terror and shame consumed me as I sat there in the dark, blood staining my clothes, feeling utterly alone and helpless.

That night, I stayed over at their house, and my friend's mom gently tried to explain what had happened to me and why I was bleeding. Her words were kind, but I barely heard them through the fog of trauma and shame. I lay awake all night in their spare room, my body still aching, convinced I was dying - both physically and inside my soul. The deep despair and loneliness felt like a physical weight crushing my chest. I was just a little girl desperately wanting to be loved, looking for any kind of positive attention I wasn't getting at home. This man had spotted my vulnerability, recognized my naivety, and deliberately preyed upon me like a wolf circling an injured lamb.

When I arrived home the following day, my mother hadn't even realized I hadn't come home the night before. Not a single call to check where I was or if I was safe. The entire experience only reinforced what I already believed - that I was unworthy of love, a horrible, unlovable, despicable human being who deserved whatever bad things happened to her. The shame and self-loathing were suffocating.

Back then, there was no counseling available to help process the trauma of rape. I simply had to get on with my life as best I could, burying the pain deep inside where it festered like an infected wound. I never told my mother what happened; until now, I suspect only my friend and her mother knew the truth. Life just went on, and I learned to carry it as a badge of shame and guilt, further proof that I didn't deserve to be loved.

The incident became yet another secret I carried, another wound that would shape who I became. Like so many traumas in my young life, I had no way to process what had happened or understand that I wasn't to blame. I just internalized it as further evidence of my worthlessness. The world had shown me once again that I was disposable.

But life had more trials in store, and they would come at me with brutal speed...

By this time, our family home was in a cul-de-sac in Rookwood Subdivision in Lexington, KY. A steep hill rose beside us, leading up to New Circle Road - a busy multi-lane highway divided by a median strip. The parents of one of my friends owned the Embers Motel across those rushing lanes of traffic, and we would regularly dash across to swim in their pool, waiting with pounding hearts for gaps in the endless stream of vehicles to reach the median, then pausing again before attempting the final dangerous crossing.

NEW CIRCLE ROAD, LEXINGTON KY

We had made this treacherous journey countless times before, but on one sweltering summer day, everything went horribly wrong. We had successfully navigated the first five lanes and were waiting tensely on the median, the heat from the asphalt rising around us in shimmering waves, when a police officer stopped in the third lane. He rolled down his window and began shouting at us to cross immediately, his voice militaristic and impatient. Traffic was backing up behind him, and horns were starting to blare. We were terrified and confused - taught to respect authority but knowing in our bones how dangerous this crossing could be.

Panicked and intimidated by his commands, we began to step off the median. In that moment of fear and hesitation, I lost one of my flip-flops and instinctively stopped to retrieve it - a split-second decision that would change everything. A driver far back in the queue, unaware of what was happening, suddenly accelerated into what he thought was an empty lane. Seeing the vehicle, I froze like a baby deer in headlights. He struck me at around 50mph, launching my small body 25 feet through the air. I landed on his hood before brutally bouncing onto the unforgiving pavement. The impact was so violent it ripped my bathing suit top completely off, leaving me partially exposed and broken on the scorching asphalt.

This became my second out-of-body experience - I can still clearly remember floating above the horrible scene as if held up by invisible strings in the heavy summer air. From up high, I watched my mother burst out our front door. She ran from our house up the hill, her bare feet throwing up little clouds of dirt with each desperate step toward my broken body on the ground. She had on lime green cotton shorts that made swishing sounds as she ran and a sleeveless pale pink button-down cotton shirt that stuck to her skin in the hot sun, dark patches of sweat spreading across the fabric.

The bright afternoon sun lit up every tiny detail: her feet hitting the rocky ground, her hair flying behind her like a flag in the wind, and the way everything seemed to move in slow motion, like time itself had turned thick and sticky. I could see her reach out to me, even though she was still far away. The scene burned into my memory like a photograph. Every single detail stuck in my mind as I watched from above - later on, I found out she really had been wearing exactly those clothes when the accident happened, right down to the smallest thing I saw while floating there.

I was rushed to the hospital with a severe concussion, multiple contusions covering my head and body, a fractured pelvis, and dangerous blood clots in my legs. Yet another layer of pain and trauma heaped upon this little girl's already heavy burden.

Dear God, how much more could I take? The answer lay waiting in the shadows of my future, ready to push me past every breaking point I thought I had...

CHAPTER 3

TIME TO LEAVE

We tell stories to heal the pain of living an unfair life
-Lenora Scurry-

Growing up, my life was an overabundance of chaos, overshadowed by my mother's turbulent relationships. By the time I was sixteen, she had walked down the aisle for the fourth time, marrying a man whose presence turned our home into a bigger battlefield. Their relationship was a symphony of screams and shouts, with fistfights punctuating the discord like a violent volcano.

This new stepfather brought his own baggage—a son and daughter who seemed to mirror his father's disdain and aggression. Our home was filled with a constant tension that seeped into every corner, causing everyone to walk on eggshells. I frequently found myself in the crossfire, stepping between my mother and the men who threatened her. Despite everything, she was still my mom, and some deep part of me longed for her approval, her love—a love that felt as elusive as a whisper in the wind.

One particular evening is etched in my memory with painful clarity. My mother had prepared a meal for us all, a rare attempt at normalcy. As we sat down, my stepbrother dismissed her efforts with scorn, calling the food disgusting and saying he wasn't going to eat it. His words struck her like a physical blow, igniting a fury that had long simmered beneath the surface. She hurled his plate at him, hitting him in the back of the head, and as the plate shattered on the floor, it left bits of food clinging to him like a grotesque painting. In the absurd silence that followed, his rage boiled over, and he turned on her with violence, pushing, shoving, and hammering her. My stepfather remained passive, a silent observer in the chaos, leaving me to intervene. I became the target of my stepbrother's wrath, and after the dust settled, I was left to clean up the mess both on the floor and in my own head, feeling both invisible and unappreciated as not even a word, nod, or any expression of thanks was offered.

ME BEFORE I MOVED OUT AT 16

The atmosphere in our house was suffocating, the air was always thick with hostility. It intensified the loneliness and sense of unworthiness that clung to me like a shadow. If my mother couldn't find love, what hope did I have? In hindsight, perhaps my attempts to help her only made things worse. My strong-willed nature was a constant reminder of her inability to control me, a source of her resentment and my suffering. Her daily display of verbal and physical abuse was becoming a show I no longer cared to watch.

Desperate to escape, I began sneaking out, vanishing for days at a time without anyone noticing or caring. I sought solace in the wrong places, clinging to any attention as a form of validation. The men I found were inevitably abusive, a reflection of the only kind of love I knew. I was a teenage girl adrift, searching for affection in a sea of abuse and neglect.

When my elder sister Sheri moved to Fort Myers, Florida, it seemed like a lifeline. Anything had to be better than the life I was living. I packed what little I had and followed her, hoping that the sunshine state would offer a reprieve from the shadows of my past. Initially, living with Sheri provided a glimmer of hope, a brief respite from the chaos. Even though I loved Sheri, I found this suffocating and moved in with a girl I'd just met. She lived in a party house, surrounded by temptation. The nights were long, filled with the haze of smoke and the clinking of bottles. The introduction of LSD into our gatherings was my newest temptation. Thankfully, I never went down that path, but the atmosphere took its toll, leaving me feeling more adrift than ever.

Despite all that chaos, I found a sliver of peace in my tiny apartment, a space I could call my own. It was modest, barely more than a room with a bed and a small kitchen, but it was mine. I tried to make it a home, but barely covering rent makes for a poor interior decorator. Each month was a struggle, the financial burden hanging over me like a dark cloud. It was in this vulnerable state that I met Terry.

Terry seemed like the answer to my prayers—a charming man who promised laughter and nights filled with dancing. On the surface, he was everything I thought I wanted. That illusion was soon shattered in the most horrific way. He invited me over to his house, promising a night out dancing. Another man was there, introduced as a friend who would join us. We sat and chatted while Terry made drinks. But soon, a strange and warm sensation washed over me, my limbs felt heavy, and my mind was clouded. Panic rose within me, but I was powerless to resist it.

I found myself floating above, watching helplessly as Terry and his friend violated me. The terror and confusion swirled within me, a tempest of emotions that left me paralyzed. I was caught in a vast, unseen space, unsure if I was dreaming or awake. The next morning, I woke in their bed, naked and ashamed. I snuck out of bed, dressed quickly, and went home, my mind a whirl of confusion and self-accusation. I didn't know if the rape had really happened. Had I been dreaming, or had I voluntarily participated in a threesome? I was so in denial that just two days later, I was back at Terry's house as if he was still my boyfriend and everything was fine.

Years later, I learned there was a name for the floating experiences that I had during those times of extreme trauma (The TV incident, the rape, the beatings) - an OBE, or Out of Body Experience. During intense trauma, some people describe feeling as if they've left their physical body behind. It's like being split in two: one part of you watches from above while the other remains present in the moment. This explained why my memories felt so strange and disconnected, as if I had been both observer and participant at once.

This splitting of consciousness is actually a survival mechanism, a way for the mind to protect itself during overwhelming trauma. While my physical body remained there, another part of me floated safely above, detached from the horror below. The experience left me questioning my own memories and reality - had I really been there, or was it just a nightmare? Understanding OBE years later helped me make sense of that night and why my memories seemed to exist from two different perspectives: the terrified girl in the bed and the helpless observer hovering above.

Much later, through trauma recovery therapy, I learned the truth—Terry had drugged me, and he and his friend had also definitely raped me. It was a revelation that was both devastating and liberating, freeing me from the chains of self-blame I had carried for so long.

As the relationship with Terry crumbled, I continued my search for love in all the wrong places. After more rounds of partying and sleeping with other men, I met Frank, a man who seemed to offer the stability and affection I craved. Because he was so kind and loving towards me, and as I needed the rent payment and did not want to become homeless, I moved in with him within a week, swept away by his charm and the promise of a new beginning. Looking back now, I can hardly believe my own naivety, especially after what happened with Terry. But when you're struggling to make rent, staring homelessness in the face and someone shows you kindness, it's amazing what you'll overlook.

Frank seemed perfect at first - loving, caring, someone who might finally give me the family I'd always wanted. But that dream was shattered the very first day I moved in. The abuse started immediately - daily kicks, punches to the face, and verbal attacks that cut deep. Now I understand what he did - experts call it "love bombing" - spotting a vulnerable woman and showering her with affection until she's trapped. At the time, I just felt confused and broken.

The neighbors would call the police regularly when they heard the violence. But the cops were useless - they took one look at us, a black man and a white woman, and verbally dismissed me as "white trash" who deserved whatever I got. Their prejudice became another tool in Frank's arsenal of control.

People often ask why I didn't just leave. It's a fair question, but when someone controls your money, your movements, even your thoughts - freedom becomes impossible. He took every paycheck I earned. His threats to kill me weren't empty words - I believed them completely.

For almost a year, I tried to escape. Each time, he'd be there, hiding, watching. He'd drag me back by my hair and beat me until I could barely move. Somehow, I managed to keep my job while living in constant terror. Frank drove me everywhere, turning his car into another prison. I learned to read his moods like warning signs, each expression forecasting what horror awaited me at home.

That day in the car, I saw death in his eyes. He started accusing me of sleeping with other men, claiming I "smelled like sex." No amount of explaining that I'd been at my desk all day mattered. After the third time I denied it, his fist connected with my face. The crack of my nose breaking and the warm flow of blood are sensations I can still feel today.

At home, he threw me onto the bed and tore off my panties - pink lacy ones he'd bought me himself. The irony of that detail has stayed with me all these years. He kept sniffing them, insisting he could smell evidence of my infidelity. The beating began, punctuated by demands that I confess to cheating.

The pattern became endless - he'd beat me, leave, come back, and catch me trying to escape. After the fourth time, he dragged me back inside, something in me broke. I stopped fighting. I lay there, accepting that this was probably how I was going to die. The blows continued all night, some from his fists, others from what I later learned was called a "pimp stick" - wire hangers twisted into a makeshift weapon that left distinctive welts, cuts, and bleeding across my skin.

When he finally exhausted himself, he forced me to perform oral sex. This act was the most humiliating form of control that I had experienced to this point. I was scared, furious, yet also compliant. Then he made me lie next to him, pinned under his arm and leg. The pain was unbearable. I begged to go to the hospital, but he just called me a "stupid bitch" and accused me of trying to escape. As he slept, I lay there fighting unconsciousness, truly believing these were my final hours. My family didn't even know where I was. Even if they did, they'd probably blame me for this, too, like they did for everything else. Like so many times before and after, I survived because I had no other choice - alone, terrified, but undefeated.

Through that endless night, I prayed harder than I ever had before. When morning came, survival meant just one thing - somehow getting out of my hell hole, no matter the cost.. I forced my broken body to move, got dressed, and acted like it was just another workday. Surprisingly, he drove me to work. I made it up three steps to the building before collapsing like a discarded rag doll onto the cold and unforgiving floor. The office staff was horrified and immediately called 911

The hospital staff later told me if I'd been an hour later, I most definitely would be dead due to swelling of my brain. Five days I stayed there, and Frank never showed - he knew better than to leave evidence of his handiwork. When I was released, I faced a terrible choice: homelessness or returning to Frank. A friend and her husband took me in temporarily, but Frank showed up with a gun, threatening everyone. After several days of this, they asked me to leave - they had young children to protect. I understood, but it still hurt.

In what could have been my final confrontation with Frank, I walked out onto my friend's porch; I took Frank's hand that held the gun and pressed it tightly to my own forehead. I was done being afraid. "Go ahead and pull the trigger, I refuse to be your victim anymore!" I said as I was shaking from head to toe. My actions belied my words, but I'd be damned if those words didn't muster a little bit of courage I never knew I had. All I knew is that I had rather die on my feet than live on my knees. That's when my friend's visitor, someone who would possibly turn out to be my knight in shining armor, stepped out and took the gun from Frank, beating him with it and warning him to stay away from me forever.

The road to healing was long and challenging, but I knew then that I had the power to reclaim my life. The experiences that had threatened to break me instead became the foundation of my strength, a testament to my resilience and will to survive.

CHAPTER 4

MY HERO

Wounds reveal stories that we're afraid to tell.
-Lenora Scurry-

The hospital bruises were still fading when I first really looked at David - the man who had saved me from Frank, my unrelenting tormentor. Standing in the doorway of my friend's house that day, his stance radiating quiet strength, he seemed like an answer to every prayer I'd whispered through those dark nights of terror.

David was tall and strong, and when I looked at him, I felt safe for the first time since I could remember. After everything with Frank - the beatings, the gun, nearly dying - having someone protect me felt like a blessing in disguise. Maybe this time would be different. Maybe this time, I'd found someone who could truly love me.

He had a tiny studio apartment and told me I could stay there since I had nowhere else to go. The place was small, but it felt like a fortress where nothing bad could touch me. Of course, I slept with him - back then, it was the only way I knew how to say thank you. Sex was how I survived, how I showed gratitude, the only thing I thought I had to give.

All I wanted was to be loved. I thought sex and love were the same thing in relationships. I didn't know about the other important stuff - being friends, having things in common, actually enjoying each other's company. How could I? I'd never seen that with my mom and her four husbands. Each of her marriages taught me what love wasn't but never what it was supposed to be. After a week or so of this arrangement, I noticed David would disappear without telling me where he was going. The pattern became clear - he'd slip away, sometimes for hours, sometimes for just 10-15 minutes. My stomach would knot up every time he left. I got suspicious, my intuition screaming that something wasn't right. The shorter absences bothered me the most - whoever he was seeing had to be close by.

One hot afternoon, as my suspicions grew, I decided to walk around my new neighborhood. The Florida sun beat down hard, making sweat trickle down my back as I tried to clear my head. I'd only gone a few blocks when my heart nearly stopped - there was David's truck parked in someone else's driveway just minutes from our place. His pickup was unmistakable. His vehicle was the talk of the town—a gleaming cherry red show truck, complete with smokestacks and a custom fire truck siren that announced its presence long before it arrived.

I stood there staring at it, my legs shaking. The house was small and neat, with flowers in the window boxes and kids' toys scattered across the yard. A family lived here - and somehow, David was connected to it. My hands were trembling as I walked up that driveway, but I had to know the truth. The gravel crunched under my feet with each step, seeming to echo how my world was about to crumble.

A shabbily dressed woman answered my knock on the door. When I told her I was David's girlfriend, her face changed from friendly to hard. Standing there in her doorway, she told me she was his wife, and they had two children together. The words hit me like a punch to the gut. I started stammering, trying to apologize, saying, "he never told me he was married." Before she could say anything else, David burst out of the house, his face twisted with rage I'd never seen before. He screamed at her to shut the fuck up, grabbed my arm hard enough to bruise, and practically threw me into his truck.

The drive home felt like it was forever even though it was just around the corner. The silence in that truck was so thick I could barely breathe. My mind raced with all the questions I was too scared to ask. When we got back, he tried to explain - said he wasn't really married to her, they were "just living together," and he was trying to break up with her. The words sounded hollow, but I wanted so badly to believe him. Why wouldn't I? I was young, scared, and thanks to him and his intervention, I'd just escaped Frank's abuse that nearly killed me. David was my protector, my savior - or at least that's what I desperately needed to believe.

Our life went on in that tiny apartment, but soon, there wasn't enough room for all my stuff. The place was so small we could barely move around - my photos, clothes, special keepsakes, and my favorite stereo system were taking up too much space. David suggested putting them in storage, and I thought he was being thoughtful. Looking back now, I can see how stupid I was. His idea of "storage" was a small shed in the backyard of the house he shared with his companion - a choice that would destroy everything I owned and lead to consequences I couldn't have imagined and would take me years to overcome.

He put a lock on the shed, but since there hadn't been one there before, she grew suspicious. Her reaction stripped away my illusions about his "companion"—only a girlfriend would have the power to demand such answers. I understand why she was suspicious - suddenly finding a locked shed in your own backyard would make anyone wonder what was inside. It was like putting up a big flashing neon sign saying something's not right, and she wasn't the kind of woman who was just going to just let things go.

You can probably guess what happened next. She broke the lock off the shed and found all my belongings packed in boxes. When she saw another woman's life stored away in her shed, she completely lost it. What she did next was cruel and calculated - she dug a big hole in the backyard, threw in everything that proved I existed, and set it all on fire. The flames ate up everything - my precious photos of me with my grandparents, my cards and love letters, my clothes, shoes, yearbooks, journals, and all the poetry I'd written since I was six years old. Every single thing that burned was another piece of who I was, turning to ash.

I stood there later, staring at the charred remains of my life, and couldn't help but wonder why all these seemingly unbelievable things kept happening to me. Not just once, but over and over again, like some cosmic joke I couldn't understand.

The photos of my grandparents hit me the hardest. Those precious pictures were the only proof I had that someone at some point in my life had once loved me completely without wanting anything in return. Just pure love, the kind I'd been searching for my whole life. Now, even those memories were nothing but ash and smoke mixed with the dirt of his and her backyard.

I'd survived Frank trying to kill me, escaped that nightmare only to end up here - watching another kind of death. Everything that proved who I was, everything that told my story, was gone.

But even after watching my past burn away, even after knowing for sure that David had this whole other family, I stayed with him. Looking back now, I see how desperate and broken I was. But I was trapped once again - no money, no support, nowhere to go. Just like with Frank, but different. This time, the trap was in my mind, and I believed I could love David enough to make him change. I was stuck in a prison I'd built myself, thinking this was all I deserved.

1987 was marked by significant cultural and historical moments: The stock market crashed on "Black Monday," Reagan challenged Gorbachev to "tear down this wall" at the Berlin Wall, U2 released "The Joshua Tree," and Michael Jackson's "Bad" topped charts. The world was changing, and now, happily (or so I hoped), so did I. Marriage became the next logical step. Really? What was I thinking? We decided to look for a house to call our own, something that would give us a fresh start. When we found a suitable property in Lehigh Acres, Florida, neither of us had enough money for the deposit. Swallowing my pride, I asked my mom for help. To my complete surprise, she agreed to put down the deposit, and suddenly, we were moving into a beautiful three-bedroom, two-bathroom house that felt like a dream come true.

While I threw myself into organizing our new home, my sisters, Sheri and Melissa, begrudgingly threw themselves into creating the perfect wedding, as if enough white coverings and flowers could cover the deep-rooted cracks in my miserable life. I chose a white lace gown that felt like armor - high-necked, proper, Edwardian-style, making me look like someone who deserved love. The veil floated down my back, held by delicate lace flowers and seed pearls, a crown for the princess I was pretending to be. Standing before the mirror that day, I barely recognized myself. The bruised, beaten girl who'd survived Frank was gone, replaced by someone who looked pure and untouchable. For one brief moment, I let myself believe I actually deserved this beauty, this chance at happiness.

MY WEDDING DAY AUGUST 1987

But even this magical moment couldn't escape the poison of hatred. My father's refusal to attend the wedding cut deeper than any of Frank's blows ever had. He wouldn't walk me down the aisle or even acknowledge the ceremony, declaring with vicious clarity that he wouldn't give his daughter to a person of color. The word he actually used was far uglier, dripping with generations of hate. Since he couldn't punish me or David, he wielded words like weapons instead, each syllable designed to wound and destroy.

His hatred was a stark reminder of the world we lived in - a world where love still had to fight against the darkness of prejudice. Looking at myself in that wedding gown, I made a silent promise that my children and grandchildren would never know that kind of hate. They would grow up in a world where love didn't see color, where their hearts would be free to choose without fear or shame.

CHAPTER 5

ECHOES OF LOVE AND BETRAYAL

We teach people how to treat us by the behaviors we accept.
-Lenora Scurry-

Three months after we said our vows, my body gave me the most precious gift - I was pregnant. The joy that flooded through me was pure and clean, untainted by my past. This was my chance to break every toxic cycle I'd inherited. I would be the mother I never had, give my child the love and security that had always been just out of my reach. This baby represented everything pure and good I'd ever dreamed of creating. I told myself that so many times that I hoped it would be the truth instead of the reality I was condemned to.

My father's response was as bitter as ever - he announced he wanted nothing to do with my child, his own grandchild, before she was even born. But life has a way of softening even the hardest hearts. Two years later, when he finally met my beautiful baby girl, all that hatred melted away. He fell completely in love with her, proving that sometimes love really can conquer all. On his death bed, he apologized for how he treated me throughout my life. I forgave him without hesitation, the words coming easily despite everything. I just wish we hadn't waited until those final moments to heal the wound that had shadowed our relationship for so long - all those years we can't get back, lost to prejudice, silence and pain.

Being pregnant was more than just a physical state for me; it was a hopeful opportunity to set things right and correct all the wrongs in my life through this new life growing inside me. Each doctor's visit and every little movement became a note in my pregnancy journal. I carefully recorded my baby's growth and the tiny clothes I bought. Every entry reflected a pure love that I was experiencing for the first time.

8 MONTHS PREGNANT IN FT. MEYERS FL, 1988

But while I floated in my bubble of maternal joy, David's true nature began to surface like a shark in shallow water. The man who had once been my protector turned predator. His fists found my body once again, his words cut deeper than Frank's had ever managed to do. Nothing I did was right anymore - not how I dressed, not how I walked, not how I breathed. The disappearing acts became more frequent, and that old familiar knot of dread took up permanent residence in my stomach.

As much as I prayed, hoped, desired, and wanted my thoughts to be paranoia, David's infidelity came back home to roost with a cruel and wicked vengeance. Women started calling our house, some taking cruel pleasure in describing their relationships with my husband in vivid detail. Others seemed genuinely shocked to learn he was married, their voices cracking with the same pain I'd felt standing in that other woman's doorway months before.

Through it all, only one thing kept me going - the precious life growing inside me. I would rest my hands on my swelling belly in the dark of night, whispering promises to my unborn child. Promises about the wonderful life we would have together, promises that I would be the best mother in the world. Promises I desperately hoped I could keep.

When labor started, David showed up at the hospital, but his resentment filled the delivery room like poison gas. He didn't even try to hide his displeasure at becoming a father again. But the moment they placed Kerry in my arms, nothing else mattered. She was absolute perfection - eight pounds and five ounces of pure miracle, with a head full of dark hair and the sweetest little nose I'd ever seen. Looking into her face, I felt love surge through me with an intensity that nearly knocked me breathless. I made a silent vow that nothing would ever harm this perfect little person. How naive I was to think I had that power.

A few months after Kerry's birth, I opened our mailbox on what seemed like any ordinary afternoon. Inside was a letter that shattered what was left of my illusions. David was being sued for child support - not for one child, but for two. Standing there with that paper trembling in my hands, everything clicked into place like a sick puzzle finally solved. These children had been born during our marriage, which explained his explosive rage during my pregnancy. He wasn't just unfaithful - he was creating entire families behind my back.

But the revelations weren't done tearing my world apart. Soon I discovered there were two more children beyond these - plus the two with the woman who had burned my belongings. In total, he had six children with other women, none of whom he supported or even saw, plus our Kerry. The happy family life I'd dreamed of creating was nothing but smoke and mirrors, a cruel joke played on a woman desperate enough to still believe in fairy tales.

I stayed for Kerry's sake, telling myself she deserved the kind of stable family I never had. I convinced myself that if I just loved him enough, showed him enough devotion, he would change. It was the same lie every abused woman tells herself, but this time I was dragging my innocent daughter into the darkness with me.

About a year after moving into our home, with Kerry around eight months old, things took an even more sinister turn. It started with phone calls - sometimes just breathing on the other end, sometimes explicit threats. The voices would tell us we needed to get out of the neighborhood, that if we didn't leave, we would be killed. They threatened to burn down our house, to murder my beautiful baby girl. Each call left me shaking, clutching Kerry to my chest, wondering how people could harbor such hatred in their hearts, especially for an innocent child.

OUR NEW HOME IN LEHIGH ACRES, FLORIDA

At first, we tried to dismiss the threats as empty words meant to frighten us. Then one day, we came home to find the beautiful stained glass in our front door shattered into a thousand pieces. Nothing was stolen, no other damage done - it was clearly meant as a message. We didn't call the police, trying to convince ourselves it was just random vandalism. But the next day, while David was at work and I was alone with Kerry, someone started pounding on our door. The voice outside was filled with such raw hatred it made my blood run cold: "You need to move, your kind ain't welcome round here!"

The beating on the door was so violent I thought the wood would splinter. My heart pounding, I clutched Kerry to my chest and backed away, searching frantically for an escape route. With trembling hands, I called the police, but by the time they arrived, our tormentor had vanished into the darkness, leaving only the echo of hatred behind.

That same evening, as Kerry played innocently on our living room floor, a rattlesnake appeared in our house like some biblical omen. David was gone - as usual - leaving me to face this new terror alone. Running on pure maternal instinct, I snatched Kerry up and secured her in her crib, then grabbed a shovel from the garage. My hands were shaking, but my aim was true. I killed that snake with one powerful strike, then threw its body outside. At the time, I dismissed it as just another Florida hazard. But what happened next stripped away any doubt about what was really going on.

The following morning, I stepped outside and felt my blood freeze. Our neighbors - both the one across from us and the one to our right - had erected wooden crosses facing our house during the night. Everything suddenly clicked into place with sickening clarity - the threatening calls, the shattered glass, the snake, and now these crosses. Our neighbors weren't just unfriendly; they were dangerous racists who wanted us gone.

Living there became psychological torture. The isolation made it worse - we were in a secluded location, and I was alone with Kerry most of the time while David was out doing God knows what with God knows who. Every creak made me jump; every shadow could hide a threat. I'd lie awake at night, my body tense and ready to grab Kerry and run at a moment's notice, listening for sounds of danger over my daughter's peaceful breathing.

Letting Go... A Mother's Journey

The situation had become unbearable. In desperation, I called the local newspaper - someone needed to expose what was happening. But David refused to let me pursue it, convinced it would only make things worse. When we alerted the police, our neighbors cleverly disguised their hatred. They'd hung bird feeders from the arms of those crosses, transforming their symbols of hate into seemingly innocent yard decorations. The police, either unwilling or unable to see the truth, dismissed our fears with a casual "no harm meant."

For seven miserable years, I endured David's betrayals and abuse. The parade of other women felt endless, each one leaving her mark on our lives like a series of cuts that never quite healed. They would knock boldly on our door, leave their clothes in our car like territorial flags, and call our house at all hours. Some seemed to take pleasure in destroying what little peace I had left.

The physical abuse escalated alongside his infidelity. The beatings became more frequent, the shoving more violent, the slaps harder, the name-calling more vicious. Each night, I'd curl up in bed, tears soaking my pillow, wondering how I'd ended up here again - trapped in another cycle of abuse as if Frank had been just a dress rehearsal for this deeper hell.

But having Kerry had changed something fundamental inside me. When I looked at her innocent face and saw her watching everything with those huge, trusting eyes, something fierce and protective would rise up in my chest. She deserved better than an absent, abusive father. She deserved better than watching her mother being beaten and humiliated. She deserved better than living in fear of racist neighbors who might hurt her just for existing.

The realization hit me like a thunderbolt - I had to get out, not just for me this time, but for her. This wasn't about my survival anymore; it was about breaking a cycle that had nearly destroyed me. I refused to let Kerry grow up thinking this was what love looked like.

In a moment of clarity and courage, I called my mom, who had relocated to Florida by then. Without hesitation, she came to get Kerry and me. Leaving our beautiful house was heartbreaking - it represented everything I'd dreamed of having, everything I'd tried to build. But I knew in my bones it was the right decision. This time, I wasn't just saving myself - I was saving my daughter from growing up thinking abuse was normal, that love and pain were inseparable.

A few weeks later, I returned to collect my belongings, intending to be fair despite everything - planning to leave him the basics he'd need to survive: some plates, utensils, the major appliances. After all, I reasoned, I wouldn't need a stove or refrigerator at my mother's house. Even after everything, some broken part of me still wanted to do the right thing.

But life had one more cruel lesson waiting in that mailbox. There, among the bills and junk mail, was a change of address notification for another woman. Two weeks - that's all it had taken him to replace me, to move another victim into the home I'd made. Until that moment, some naive part of me had still been clinging to hope, still believing that maybe, just maybe, he had loved me once and that we could work on it.

Walking into the house, my shock crystallized into white-hot rage when I found the other woman's lingerie spread across my bed - draped deliberately across my own comforter like a declaration of victory. The sheer audacity of it hit me like a ton of bricks, and suddenly I was back in that smoke-filled yard, watching my possessions burn. But this time, something different ignited inside me - not the helpless anger of before, but a cold, calculated fury.

Looking around at everything in that house - every stick of furniture, every appliance, every dish and towel that I had bought while he contributed nothing but pain - something finally snapped inside me. All those years of being beaten down, cheated on, made to feel worthless... it ended here. I marched straight to the phone and called for a U-Haul truck.

I took EVERYTHING. Not just the furniture and appliances, but every last scrap of domestic life. I stripped that house like locusts stripping a field - took the shower curtain rings, the soap from the soap dishes, even the half-empty toilet paper rolls. By the time I finished, those bare rooms echoed with emptiness, just like his promises. Driving away in that loaded U-Haul, I felt a savage satisfaction knowing he and his new woman would have to start from scratch, just like I had so many times before.

Mom had taken Kerry and me into her home, but I knew we couldn't stay there long-term. The wounds from my childhood were still too raw, the dynamics too complicated. I needed to find work, but job hunting with a small child presented unique challenges. After everything I'd been through, the thought of leaving Kerry with strangers made my heart ache. I couldn't bear the idea of her spending her days in some daycare center where I'd only see her in the evenings - not when I'd fought so hard to protect her from becoming another generation of broken women in our family.

Then, like a gift from heaven, I was offered a position as director of a daycare center. The timing felt almost miraculous - Kerry could come with me to work, staying close where I could protect her, while I earned a living. For the first time in years, the pieces of my shattered life seemed to be falling into place.

I threw myself into the work with everything I had, loving those children as if they were my own. Each little face that came through those doors became precious to me - I saw in them the childhood I never had, the innocence I was determined to protect. But life had other plans. About a year after I started, the company that owned the business sold it to new owners who cared more about profit margins than children's wellbeing.

The changes they wanted to implement went against everything I believed in - everything I knew these children needed. I couldn't compromise my principles, not when it came to kids. Before I left, though, I contacted all the parents to explain the situation. Their response stunned me - they trusted me with their children and asked if I would consider opening my own daycare center.

Their faith in me was transformative. For someone who had spent her life being told she was worthless, having parents trust me with their most precious possessions was overwhelming. So I did what seemed impossible - I found a cute, well-maintained house on a street called - if you can believe it - Happy Lane. The irony of that name wasn't lost on me. I converted half of it into a daycare center thanks to the donations from the same people that entrusted their children to me, and Kerry (who was three by then) and I lived in the other half. Finally, I had created exactly what I'd always wanted - a way to take care of my daughter by myself while making a living.

FOUR GENERATIONS (GRANDMA MARY, MOTHER EVELYN, ME, KERRY)

Running that daycare center became one of the most rewarding and challenging experiences of my life. I worked with the government to provide care for children from underprivileged homes, and what I saw broke my heart daily. Many of these kids came to me carrying deep emotional and mental scars that manifested in difficult behaviors. I remember one little boy who would repeatedly bang his head on the floor - it was as if he was trying to use physical pain to block out some deeper emotional anguish. Looking at him, I saw myself at that age, trying to cope with pain too big for a child to handle.

The parents often presented challenges that tested my patience and principles. Despite our clear closing time of 6 PM, many would routinely leave their children until 7 or 8 in the evening, showing no regard for my own time or family needs. I understood their struggles - many were single parents working multiple jobs - but their disrespect for boundaries wore me down day by day.

The most extreme case was a mother who left her eight-month-old baby with me for TWO WEEKS! After my repeated calls went unanswered, my heart breaking for this abandoned infant, I had no choice but to contact the authorities. These situations tore at my soul - I couldn't help but see myself in these neglected children, couldn't help but wonder if someone had intervened for me when I was young, would my life have been different?

By the time Kerry turned five and was ready to start school, I was completely burned out. Running the daycare, being a single mother, and managing a household by myself had taken its toll. I was exhausted down to my bones. The emotional weight of caring for these troubled children while trying to give Kerry the stable, loving home I'd never had was becoming too much to bear. Each night, after Kerry was asleep, I'd sit in the darkness of our little house on Happy Lane, feeling anything but happy.

In a moment of desperation, I called my older sister Melissa, who had relocated to Georgia along with my mom. I poured out my exhaustion and frustration, practically begging for advice and help. She begrudgingly offered to let Kerry and me stay with her and her husband for a while, giving us a chance to start fresh. Her reluctance was clear in her voice, but at that point, I was too desperate to care.

Any small thing my family did for me did not come without a price. Although I was excited about the move, another part of me dreaded what I would have to endure while staying with my sister. Her snide remarks, her looks of disdain, her passive-aggressive behavior would all culminate into more self loathing and doubt. We packed up and left Florida behind, heading to Georgia with hope for a better future. Kerry started school, and with her taken care of during the day, I was finally able to focus on finding a job for myself. Within six months, I landed a great position at a photography studio that paid well enough for me to rent a small duplex apartment for Kerry and me.

Working those long hours at the studio wasn't easy, but for the first time in years, I felt truly hopeful. I thought my dark days were finally behind me. I was happy, Kerry was happy, and it seemed like we'd finally found our path to a better life.

Working at the photography studio and building our new life in Georgia felt like finally stepping into sunshine after years of storms. Kerry was at school, I was earning good money, and we had our own place - all the pieces I'd dreamed of were falling into place. But life has a way of teaching us that "happily ever after" is more complicated than fairy tales would have us believe. While I kept telling myself everything was fine, there was one shadow I couldn't quite shake - Kerry's father. His absence was like a hole in our lives that grew larger as Kerry got older. Watching her notice other kids with their dads at the park or school events made my heart ache in ways I hadn't expected. I told myself I could fix this too, just like I'd fixed everything else. But some broken things can't be repaired, no matter how hard we try.

CHAPTER 6

THE DARKNESS RETURNS

Even in the darkest of times hope can help you prevail
-Lenora Scurry-

My daughter and I were doing OK; we had our own place, I had a decent income, and she was settled at school. Each morning as I drove to work at the photography studio, I'd repeat those words like a mantra, trying to convince myself that everything was fine. But in the quiet moments, when the house was still and Kerry was asleep, the truth would creep in like shadows at dusk. The fly in the ointment was her father, who refused to have anything to do with her. That hadn't been too much of an issue when she was tiny - babies don't ask questions about absent parents - but as she grew and saw all her friends spending time with their dads, Kerry naturally yearned for the same. My heart would splinter watching her little face fall every time she saw another father pushing his child on the swings or attending a school event. The weight of her longing pressed against my chest like a 45 pound barbell plate. How could I fix this? What could I do?

The exhausting eight-hour drives to Fort Myers, Florida became my answer - a desperate attempt to bridge the gap between father and daughter. I'd pack us into the car before dawn, watching Kerry's excited face in the rearview mirror as highway markers ticked past like a countdown to disappointment. We'd check into whatever cheap motel we could afford, the worn carpets and faded wallpaper matching my increasingly frayed hopes. Then would come the call - my trembling fingers dialing his number, praying this time would be different.

Sometimes he would show up, and Kerry's face would light up like Christmas morning, making every mile worth it. But more often, there would just be silence on the other end of the line, and I'd have to watch my daughter's hopes crumble yet again, her small shoulders slumping as she curled into herself on the scratchy motel bedspread and cried for what seemed like hours.

Then he began to race motorcycles professionally in Commerce, Georgia. The irony was almost too cruel to bear - he would drive right past our exit to get to the racetrack, yet he couldn't be bothered to stop and see his daughter. Instead, I would pack us up again and drive Kerry to another cheap motel near the races. He never offered me a penny toward these visits, not for gas, not for the room, not for food - yet he would spend literally thousands on his racing hobby. His priorities were clear in his actions: motorcycles meant more to him than his own child.

The exhaustion of trying to maintain a relationship between Kerry and her father was crushing me. Each disappointing visit, each time he chose racing over his daughter, each mile driven in vain - it all took its toll. I could see the light dim a little more in Kerry's eyes every time her father failed to show up. The weight of his constant rejection settled over us like a heavy blanket, suffocating our hopes.

By the time Kerry was six, I was working hard and earning good money at the photography studio so when my mother and sister Melissa offered to take Kerry to church with them one Sunday, it seemed like a reasonable solution. I had only one requirement, one rule that I made absolutely clear: Kerry was not to go to the bathroom alone. The church was massive, with winding hallways and multiple floors where a child could easily get lost. Or worse. That "or worse" whispered in the back of my mind like a premonition I tried desperately to ignore.

The irony of what happened next still haunts me. While Melissa wouldn't let her own four-year-old daughter use the bathroom alone, my explicit instruction about Kerry was absolutely ignored. My six-year-old daughter was allowed to go by herself. Those few minutes would change our lives forever.

In that fluorescent-lit church bathroom, my baby girl became prey. A sixteen-year-old boy from the congregation - someone who should have been trustworthy in a house of God - followed her inside. His hand clamped over her mouth, silencing her terrified screams, as he dragged her down the carpeted hallway to an empty classroom. The sacred quiet of the church service continued above, oblivious to the horror unfolding below.

Inside that classroom, he sexually assaulted my six-year-old daughter. The violation was methodical, calculated - forcing her to perform oral sex, then performing it on her. She was just six years old. Six. The same age I had been when trauma first visited my own life. But my brave, fierce little girl found strength I never had - she fought back, punching him hard in the head. Her screams finally pierced the sanctity of the church service as she ran, her terror echoing off the vaulted ceilings.

I was just finishing work when my mother's call came: "Kerry's been molested. You need to get to the church right away." Those words hit me like a prize fighters fists. The drive there exists as a blank space in my memory - one moment I was at work, the next I was fully into my third out of body experience and was floating above the crowd at the church, watching my body move through the sea of people, hearing my voice shouting "Where's Kerry? Where's my baby?"

It seemed surreal and kind of ironic "angelically" floating above all the chaos, watching as police officers asked questions, congregation members standing around talking, as church elders conversed. The thing that brought me back down to earth was the sight of my baby girl's bruised little cheek and the tears streaming down her face. As I was coming back to reality, the police asked Kerry and I questions that neither could fully answer.

Days passed at a snails pace. But soon, the investigation revealed something even more horrifying - this wasn't the boy's first offense. His grandfather was in prison for molesting him and other children. He knew exactly what he was doing to my daughter.

One of the detectives pulled me aside, his face grim. His words still haunt me: if Kerry hadn't managed to escape, the boy likely would have raped and killed her to cover up his crime. Even now, decades later, those words send ice through my veins.

The investigation uncovered an even darker truth about the church's complicity. The boy had powerful connections within the congregation - his aunt was an administrator. She had the audacity to call me, warning me to drop the investigation because she was worried about her reputation. I remember sobbing into the phone, trying to explain through my tears that I wasn't the one investigating - this was a police matter now. But she didn't care about that distinction, or about what had happened to my six-year-old daughter.

I knew in my gut that the church would try to sweep this under the rug, but I was determined not to let them drive us away. I decided we would return to that church. Perhaps I thought we could find healing there, that surely a house of God would embrace and support us in our darkest hour. I couldn't have been more wrong.

The reception we received was beyond cold - it was cruel, calculated, and devastating. People who had once embraced us would literally see us coming and hurry out through another door to avoid us. The same congregation that had shared meals with us, prayed with us, and sung hymns beside us now treated us like we were plague carriers. Not a single person - not one - reached out to offer support or comfort to a traumatized six-year-old girl and her shattered mother.

Instead, I was asked to leave the choir until I could "get myself together" - as if my daughter's assault was some minor inconvenience I needed to quickly overcome. We were treated like we were the criminals - a mother and her abused six-year-old daughter were somehow blamed for the actions of a sexual predator. The victim-blaming was so blatant it took my breath away.

The betrayal by the church cut deeper than any physical wound. These were people who preached love and protection, yet they turned their backs on us when we needed them most. Even the pastor - the man who was supposed to be our spiritual shepherd - never once visited us at home or even made a phone call to check on mine and Kerry's well-being.

The next "feeling" I expressed emerged from a place beyond tears - a hollow, gutted landscape where pain had scorched everything silent. I explained to my mother this had been one of my deepest fears. I always diligently prayed over Kerry, begging God for protection with every fiber of my being.

Why did He allow this to happen?

My mother's eyes hardened, her condescending voice cutting through my grief. "Well, you DO know that the bible says 'For the thing which I greatly feared is come upon me, and that which I was afraid of is come unto me.' " - Job 3:25

I looked up, my voice a wounded whisper, "Really? You're going to use scripture to blame me for what happened to Kerry?" The weight of her words once again brought the feelings that I had been the scapegoat my entire life, a perpetual target for her disappointment and disdain, with every misstep pinned squarely on my shoulders. I had grown accustomed to the sting of her accusations, each one a dagger that dug deeper into my already fragmented heart, as if no matter the situation, the blame was always mine to bear. What happened next was the universe's chance to twist that knife into me just a little bit deeper.

The event that day was blasted all over the news. Some people who saw what happened suggested I sue the church, but my pastor and family quickly shot that down. They wielded Bible verses like weapons against me, particularly Ephesians 4:31: "Let all bitterness and wrath and anger and clamor and slander be put away from you, along with all malice." Their words dripped with sanctimonious judgment as they demanded to know how I could dare take another Christian to court before non-believers. "How can they render justice if they don't believe in the God of justice?" (I Corinthians 6:6)

The pain just kept deepening, like an already gaping wound being torn open, never allowing any room for healing. I felt completely alone, drowning while everyone watched from the shore of their self-righteous judgment. Every Sunday, we'd force ourselves to return to that church, and people who once embraced me would literally turn and walk away, their faces twisted with disgust. These were the same people who used to wrap me in warm hugs, who I'd lifted my voice within the choir, and who I'd worked alongside in women's ministry. Now, they treated us like we carried some contagious spiritual disease.

The church leaders pressured me not to get counseling for Kerry, claiming it wasn't God's will - that prayer and fasting alone would heal everything. As if somehow divine intervention would magically erase the trauma of sexual assault from a six-year-old's psyche. I listened to them because I trusted them, believed in their spiritual authority. Now, looking back, self-loathing consumes me for not getting her the professional help she desperately needed right away. A child needs more than just prayers after being violated in God's own house.

So we tried to handle it ourselves, suffocating under the weight of silence and shame. But we weren't handling it at all. We were just burying it deeper, letting it fester like an untreated wound beneath the surface. The damage would eventually surface in ways I couldn't have imagined, setting us on a path that would ultimately tear us apart.

I still had to work - bills don't stop coming just because your world falls apart. Every morning, I'd force myself out of bed, get Kerry to school, and somehow make it through another workday. But I was like a zombie, just going through the motions, my body present while my mind remained trapped in that church bathroom where my baby girl's innocence was stolen.

When I got home, I couldn't do anything. I mean nothing at all. I'd sit there in the growing darkness, staring into nothingness while our home crumbled around us. Trash piled up in every corner, empty food containers breeding maggots in the kitchen. The bathtub grew so filthy we couldn't even use it - a far cry from the immaculate home I'd once taken such pride in maintaining. But I couldn't summon the energy to care anymore. The weight of failure - of not protecting my daughter - pressed down on me like a never ending physical force.

I started ordering takeout for every meal because I couldn't make myself cook. The empty boxes would accumulate, but I couldn't even find the strength to throw them away. Everything just kept deteriorating, spiraling deeper into chaos. Looking back now, I recognize I was in the depths of severe depression, watching helplessly as mine and my baby's life disintegrated in slow motion, powerless to stop it.

The assault on Kerry tore my already dysfunctional family apart at the seams. My elder sister and mom kept blaming each other for letting Kerry go to the bathroom alone that day. They fought so viciously that my mom finally packed up and moved back to Kentucky, unable to take it anymore. That was just like her - she never wanted to deal with anything complicated in her life. Once she left, I had even less family to turn to and still no church to seek comfort in.

I felt so lost. The darkness just kept getting deeper and deeper. I started thinking about killing myself. The only thing that stopped me was Kerry - I couldn't leave her alone in this world. Then, my mind went to an even darker place. I bought sleeping pills and would lie in bed thinking about giving them to both of us. I imagined us lying together, her safe in my arms as we drifted away to somewhere better than this. The pain was so unbearable I couldn't see any other way out.

This went on for weeks, then months. The thoughts of ending it all consumed me, but somehow we survived. After about a year, I started functioning more like a normal person again. But I never really got over what happened. Even now, the guilt eats at me like acid - she was my little girl, and I wasn't there to protect her. I carry that weight every single day, a burden that never lightens.

Once again abandoned by everyone who should have cared, I turned to writing to get my feelings out. It's strange - I didn't realize until I started writing this book that both Kerry and I had life-changing traumas happen to us when we were six years old. Sometimes, I wonder how different our lives might have been without those dark times hitting us so young. Maybe my childhood would have stayed the same since things were already bad before my electrocution, but Kerry and I might have had a better shot at happiness if the molestation hadn't happened. Or maybe that's just wishful thinking from a mother's broken heart.

Life went on for both of us, including the occasional visit with her dad. Kerry was eleven months old when we left David, and despite his behavior, I still tried to get him to spend time with his daughter. The visits were hit and miss, mostly miss.

When Kerry was around ten, David suggested something that made my heart soar and tremble - he'd pick her up on his way to the motorcycle races in Commerce. Though anxiety gnawed at my stomach since he'd never offered anything like this before, I couldn't say no when I saw Kerry's face light up like a sunrise. She bounced around the house for days, planning what she'd pack, talking non-stop about spending time with her daddy, her eyes sparkling with a hope that both warmed and terrified me.

We went shopping and bought her this little pink suitcase covered in sunflowers. She picked it out herself, beaming with such pure joy it almost hurt to witness. Those sunflowers were her favorite - just like her, they always seemed to be reaching for the light, turning their faces toward warmth no matter how dark the shadows. She packed that suitcase like it held all her dreams, folding each piece of clothing with such tender care, making sure everything was perfect for her daddy. Each item placed inside was weighted with her desperate desire for his love.

The morning he was supposed to come, she was up before dawn, perched by the window in her very best outfit, that little pink suitcase sitting beside her like a faithful companion. Hour after hour ticked by. No David. My stomach twisted into knots as I watched her face slowly transform - from bright excitement to worried anticipation to devastating heartbreak. Still, she wouldn't give up. "He's just running late, Mom. He'll be here soon," she'd whisper, her voice getting weaker with each passing hour.

But he never came. My baby girl cried herself to sleep that night, clutching that damn pink suitcase like it was the last piece of her father she had left. Her tiny fingers gripped the handle so tight her knuckles were white; each sob that shook her little body was like a dagger to my heart. As her mother, I had to watch helplessly as my child learned her first brutal lesson about abandonment, unable to shield her from this pain that would shape her future in ways I couldn't yet imagine.

Every time someone knocked on the door, or the phone rang over the next three weeks, Kerry would leap up with such desperate hope it made my heart crack. "That's my daddy, that's my daddy!" Her voice would ring out, trembling with anticipation that never dimmed, even as disappointment after disappointment piled up. The light in her eyes would flare brightly for that brief, precious moment, then fade into shadows when she realized it wasn't him - again.

I watched my daughter's faith in her father die one unanswered knock at a time. Each time the phone rang or someone came to the door, I'd see that same cruel cycle - hope blazing to life in her face, only to be extinguished moments later. The way her shoulders would slump, how her smile would crumple at the edges before disappearing completely - it was like watching a flower wilt in real-time. As her mother, I felt utterly helpless, unable to shield her from this slow death of trust and love.

She wouldn't let me unpack that little pink suitcase, clutching it like a lifeline. "No mom, because my dad's gonna come, my dad's gonna come," she'd insist through her tears, her voice getting smaller each time. Those words still haunt my dreams sometimes. That cheerful sunflower-covered suitcase became a symbol of every broken promise, every disappointment, every time her father chose not to be her father.

It took him three weeks to finally call her. Three weeks of watching my daughter sleep with that packed suitcase next to her bed, waiting for a father who couldn't be bothered to show up. Each night, I'd stand in her doorway after she fell asleep, watching her tiny form curled protectively around that suitcase like it was a lifeline to the father she desperately wanted to believe in. Those sunflowers on the case seemed to mock us now, their cheerful faces a stark contrast to the darkness of abandonment.

That's when I knew - really knew - that I had to protect her from more disappointment. The truth hit me with crushing clarity: if he wanted to be a father to her, he'd have to make that choice himself. You can't force someone to love their child. Trust me, I know. I'd learned that lesson the hard way, first as a daughter yearning for my own father's love, and now as a mother watching history repeat itself through my baby girl's tears.

The cruelest part wasn't just his absence—it was the hope he left behind—hope that slowly poisoned her heart as she waited for a father who treated her love like an afterthought. No child should have to learn so young that sometimes the people who are supposed to love them the most can hurt them the deepest.

Time has a way of clarifying things that are too painful to see clearly. This period in our lives seemed to be the beginning of our end. Like a crack spreading across a windshield - at first, just a hairline fracture you might miss if the light didn't hit it just right, then suddenly it's spiderwebbing in all directions, and there's nothing you can do to stop it. My sweet little girl slowly disappeared. In her place stood someone I no longer recognized - distant, angry, hurting.

CHAPTER 7

MISTAKES MADE WITH GOOD INTENTIONS

Mistakes can be our greatest teachers, provided we are willing to learn from them.
-Lenora Scurry-

When I stopped being the go-between for Kerry and her father, my worst fears materialized - he simply vanished from her life. In those quiet moments when the house is eerily still, I wonder if his absence set her on such a troubled path. The pain of watching my little girl yearn for a daddy who chose not to stay still echoes in my heart, even after all these years. It's one of those questions that keeps a mother awake at night, searching for answers that never come.

The guilt settles over me like a familiar weight. Here I was, feeling responsible for their broken relationship when I'd spent years trying to keep it alive - driving endless hours for visits he'd often skip, making excuses for his absence until I ran out of words. That's what mothers do, isn't it? Take on blame that isn't rightfully ours, carrying burdens that should never have been ours to bear. This guilt layered on top of what I already carried about the church incident - my failure to protect her from that assault. My response was to try making everything else in her life perfect, as if enough toys and treats could somehow fill the empty spaces in her heart like food was the answer to fill the empty spaces in mine.

My own weight became a constant reminder of my struggles. Close to 400 pounds, I felt trapped in a body that betrayed me, a vessel weighed down by anxiety and the shadows of my past. I was caught in a cycle, using food as a balm for the emotional wounds that seemed to multiply with every passing day. My health spiraled downwards, a reflection of the turmoil within. I tried to convince myself that if I could just fix my physical self, perhaps the rest of my life would follow suit. But every attempt at dieting or exercise felt like a futile battle against an ever-looming darkness, leaving me more exhausted and defeated. As I faced the mirror, I didn't just see the weight; I saw the burdens I carried, the guilt that wrapped around me like a suffocating shroud, and the unresolved pain that I had yet to confront.

THE RESULT OF PUTTING FOOD FIRST

In the midst of this turmoil, I threw myself into being both mom and dad, determined Kerry would never feel the rejection or want that had marked my childhood. I believed that by stepping into this dual role, I could shield her from the pain I had endured, even as I struggled to confront my own demons. I'd rush in to fix any problem when trouble came, thinking I was showing love. Instead, I was teaching her that she never had to face life's challenges head-on.

Without meaning to, I created exactly what my mother would have sneered at - a child who expected the world on a silver platter. When I occasionally tried to say no, Kerry would explode, screaming that as her mother, it was my job to give her whatever she wanted. The sweet little girl I'd raised was transforming into someone I barely recognized, and I felt powerless to stop it.

Looking back now, with the wisdom of years, I can see how badly I messed up. All those material things, all that rushing to smooth her path - what Kerry really needed was boundaries and guidance. But how could I know? My own childhood had been a masterclass in how not to parent. I was working from a broken blueprint, trying my best to build something better.

The distance between us grew wider during her teenage years. Our house became a battlefield, with every day bringing new conflicts. Kerry started dating guys who were trouble with a capital T - just like I had at her age. The parallel scared me to death, but whenever I tried to talk to her about it, we'd end up screaming at each other. We were trapped in a cycle of pain, both wanting to connect but somehow always missing each other.

My family didn't help matters. I remember when my sisters took their kids to Six Flags, deliberately excluding Kerry. When she found out, she cried all day. Their excuse - they assumed I couldn't afford it - was just that, an excuse. They didn't want us there, plain and simple. Watching my daughter face the same kind of family rejection I'd grown up with broke something inside me and made me furious.

At nineteen, Kerry moved states away with yet another bad news boyfriend. History repeated itself in the worst way - he turned out to be violently abusive. Sometimes I wonder if there's something in our family's DNA that draws us to these destructive relationships. My mom, me, and now Kerry - three generations of women looking for love but finding only pain.

The call came at 3 AM - a stranger's voice crackling through the phone line: "Are you Kerry's mom?" When I confirmed, they didn't mince words: "You need to come and get her, or this guy is going to kill her."

Something primal awakened in me - that fierce, unstoppable instinct that doesn't stop to think about consequences. Here I come Baby Girl! Momma Bear was busy gathering her weapons like I was heading into battle: my trusted gun tucked into its holster, pepper spray in my pocket, and a solid baseball bat in my hands. Looking back, it seems crazy that I didn't think to call the police, but since I had already called my sisters to see if their husbands would go with me, which was met with a resounding "NO" because they didn't want to get caught in the middle, I knew I was again going at this alone. Rational thought wasn't exactly my strong suit when my baby was in danger.

I called Kerry and demanded they meet me in a business parking lot in Alabama - no way was I walking into his territory blind. The drive was a blur of rage and fear, my mind conjuring up every possible scenario I might face.

When they pulled up, my heart stopped. There was my baby girl, my Kerry, looking so small and broken. The sight of her made me physically sick - her face was a mess of dried blood, crusted dark around a gash where that bastard had smashed a heavy beer mug into her head. Four months pregnant with my grandchild, and this monster had treated her like a punching bag. The blood wasn't just on her face - it had dripped down onto her shirt, telling the story of just how hard he'd hit her.

Something snapped in me. I grabbed that baseball bat, feeling its weight in my hands, and faced down her abuser. I taunted him, my voice dripping with contempt. "Come on, tough guy - try hitting someone who can hit back!" I called him every name I could think of, deliberately provoking him, daring him to make a move. Looking back, it was incredibly reckless - he could have overpowered both of us easily. But there's something about bullies - when someone stands up to them and shows no fear, they often back down. And he did, shrinking away from this middle-aged mama with a bat and murder in her eyes.

We loaded Kerry's belongings - everything she owned stuffed into trash bags and broken boxes - into my car. Each item told its own story of a life interrupted, of dreams gone wrong. The whole time, I kept one hand near my pepper spray, watching him in my peripheral vision, ready for any sudden moves.

Back in Georgia, I bought us a house in Jonesboro, thinking having Kerry under my roof would ease my constant worry. But her ex wasn't done with us. The harassment was relentless - constant phone calls at all hours, false police reports, accusations that kept local law enforcement showing up at our door. Every ring of the phone, every knock at the door set our nerves on edge.

Our relationship remained volatile - maybe because I couldn't stop trying to protect her, even though she was about to become a mother herself. She saw my help as control, while I saw it as love. When Bradley, my grandson, was born, I prayed things would get better. But Bradley's father kept up his harassment, demanding "well checks" while never offering a dime of support. It was like watching my own story play out all over again - another absent father, another cycle of pain.

As I sit behind my laptop, I can't help but feel a knot in my stomach watching my daughter struggle. It hits me hard—another absent father, another cycle of hurt playing out right in front of me. I remember what it felt like when my dad walked out on us, leaving my mom to pick up the pieces. That emptiness never really goes away, does it? Today, seeing Kerry deal with that same longing for a father figure who doesn't care makes me feel both angry and helpless. No matter how much I tried to protect her, I couldn't stop the pain she's going through. Each time she cries, each time she shuns me away, each time she calls me names and spews hate and nasty words my way, it echoes my own tears from years ago, and I can't shake the worry that we were both forever trapped in a pattern that feels impossible to escape. I'm watching my past unfold again, and the weight of it crushes me, however I must move on.

I saw so much of myself in Kerry—her longing for validation, that desperate need to be loved by a man, any man, even if he didn't deserve her. It was a painful reflection of my own past, memories flooding back of nights spent chasing after affection, believing that love was something I had to earn. I recognized the trauma driving her choices because I had lived it too, feeling unworthy and desperate for connection. I wanted to pull her close, to shield her from the mistakes I had made, but I often felt like I was fighting an uphill battle. Understanding the problem was one thing; I could see the patterns, the way she gravitated towards the wrong guys like moths to a flame, but knowing how to fix it was an entirely different matter. I tried to guide her, to share my experiences, but every time I reached out, it felt like I was pushing her further away. Sometimes, despite my fierce love as a mother, I had to confront the painful truth that love alone isn't enough to break these deeply ingrained patterns. It was a hard lesson to learn, realizing that no matter how much I cared, I couldn't change her choices or protect her from the heartaches that seemed to follow us both. Watching her struggle brought a mix of heartache and frustration, knowing that she was caught in a cycle that I wanted so desperately to help her escape, yet feeling powerless to do so.

CHAPTER 8

THERE'S ALWAYS LIGHT AT THE END OF THE TUNNEL

Looking for love in all the wrong places?
Look inside
-Lenora Scurry-

My grandson Bradley was only a few months old when Kerry found him - another man who would change our lives forever. He lived nearby, fresh out of prison with nothing to his name: no money, no job, no car. Just another drug addict living with his parents. I watched helplessly as my daughter fell for him, my heart breaking because I understood all too well what she was really looking for. Love. The same desperate search for connection that had driven me when I was younger.

I tried reasoning with her, my words careful but urgent. "This relationship isn't healthy, Kerry. You deserve so much better than falling back into the same pattern you had with Bradley's father." But she wouldn't hear it. To her, I was just being controlling, interfering in her chance at happiness. How could I make her understand that I saw myself in her choices - the same mistakes, the same pain waiting to happen?

As the weeks passed, Kerry began leaving her tiny son with me more and more often, disappearing for days with this man. Don't get me wrong - I cherished every moment with my grandson. But watching my daughter leave her baby all the time stirred something angry and frightened inside me. A mother should be there for her child. I knew that truth in my bones.

I had one rule: he wasn't allowed in my house. At first, Kerry would try to sneak him in, testing my boundaries. Then they stopped pretending altogether, his presence an invasion as he walked through my front door like he owned it. My home - the safe haven I'd worked so hard to create - began to feel like enemy territory.

Things escalated until I had no choice but to tell Kerry she needed to leave. Her response was explosive - she stormed down my hallway, systematically smashing the glass in every family photo on the wall. Each crack of glass felt like a physical blow. I called the police, but it made little difference. He kept coming around, and together, they turned my life into a never-ending nightmare - stealing from me, cursing at me, treating my home like it was worthless.

Watching my sweet, loving daughter transform into this angry stranger was like dying by inches. Every day brought a new heartbreak, another piece of her slipping away into the chaos of trauma-driven choices. In my desperation to cope, I found myself sliding back into old habits, seeking numbness in substances I thought I'd left behind. The bitter irony wasn't lost on me - here I was, falling back into addiction while watching my daughter repeat similar patterns.

I loved Kerry and Bradley with every fiber of my being - still do - but my life had become unbearable. One day, after reaching my absolute breaking point, I bought a twelve-pack of beer and sleeping pills, checked into a small hotel, and prepared to end it all. Before leaving, I'd spoken to my friend Jeannie, telling her where I was going just to ease her mind. Looking back, I think some part of me was crying out for help.

At the hotel, I changed into my bathing suit and lowered myself into the hot tub, the beer and pills within easy reach. I planned to drift off in that warm water and never wake up. But life, it seems, wasn't finished with me yet. Within minutes, there was a knock at the door - police officers responding to a call about someone who might be suicidal. I denied everything, of course, but they spotted the pills and alcohol. They tried to convince me to get help, but I insisted I'd changed my mind. Eventually, they left.

Then Jeannie called. She admitted she'd been the one to call the police, having sensed something wrong in my voice earlier. That dear friend saved my life that day. Without her intervention, I would have taken those pills, drunk that beer, and let the warm water become my final resting place. I would have found what I thought was peace, leaving behind a legacy of pain for my family.

When I returned home, the state of my house nearly sent me running back to that hotel room. It was filthy, chaotic - a physical manifestation of how far things had deteriorated. If it hadn't been for Bradley, I might have turned right around, went back to the hotel and tried again. But I stayed, for him. My home had become a place of fear. There were nights I was afraid to fall asleep, terrified of what my own daughter and her boyfriend might do. How wrong is that - to be scared in your own home, of your own child?

Letting Go... A Mother's Journey

Friends urged me to leave, but I felt trapped. I had no money, no job - I was spending my days caring for Bradley so Kerry could work sometimes and party sometimes. Finally, one friend made a suggestion that seemed impossible at first: sell everything, including the house, and move to a shelter. They feared for my safety - both mental and physical - if I stayed in that environment.

Thanks to a vivid imagination and stories I had read when I was younger, the thought of living in a shelter filled me with sheer horror. Thankfully, the shelter was nothing like I'd imagined. While clean and well-organized, it still felt like rock bottom. I spent the first two days locked in my room, crying until I had no tears left. How had my life come to this? But sometimes hitting bottom is what forces you to look up.

A shelter therapist reached out to me, and her words became my lifeline. "There's always light at the end of the tunnel," she said, "no matter how dark things seem right now." Then came the news that I only had thirty days to stay. That deadline terrified me at first - how could anyone rebuild a life in just thirty days? But sometimes pressure creates diamonds.

I threw myself into following every shelter rule and found a job quickly. The shelter even provided transportation, and I worked every shift I could get my hands on, seven days a week if possible. I saved every penny like my life depended on it - because it did. Twenty days in, I had enough for a used Toyota Camry. It wasn't much, but it was freedom.

Then came another blessing. Through a friend's newspaper search, I found a "mother-in-law" apartment - one bedroom, one bath, with its own entrances. The location took my breath away, with views that seemed to speak directly to my wounded soul. The owners, Ralph and Kathy, weren't just landlords - they became angels in human form, welcoming me with open arms. This small space would become my sanctuary, my healing place.

THE VIEW FROM MY SANCTUARY

I moved in with nothing but a cheap mattress on the floor and the few clothes I'd kept. That first night alone, lying on that mattress, the reality of everything hit me hard. I cried until my chest ached. Thoughts of ending it all crept back in, but something kept me going - maybe the kindness of Ralph and Kathy, maybe the support of my friends, maybe just pure stubbornness.

The hardest part - the part that kept me awake night after night - was not knowing where Kerry and Bradley were living. I'd sold my house out from under them, a decision that still visits me in my nightmares. Every time I close my eyes, I can hear the echo of their footsteps leaving that house for the last time. The weeks that followed were pure torture. I'd find myself wondering if my grandson had enough to eat. Was he warm enough at night? Did he have a proper bed? Every mother knows that special kind of agony - when your child is out there somewhere, maybe suffering, and you can't reach them. The worry gnawed at me like a physical pain, settling deep in my bones. I wanted so desperately to help, to talk to her, to hold my grandson just once and tell him his Gammi loved him more than life itself. But Kerry saw every outstretched hand as a fist of control, every worried phone call as an attack. Each attempt to bridge the gap between us only seemed to push her further away, until that gap felt wide enough to swallow us both whole.

When Kerry got pregnant again, this time with my granddaughter Misty, my heart shattered anew. She was still with that same boyfriend, trapped in an endless cycle of addiction and poverty. Despite his meth addiction, his refusal to work, and his habit of stealing Kerry's money, they somehow managed to find a place together. But they could barely keep the lights on or put food on the table. I'd bring groceries whenever I could - watching my daughter and grandchildren go hungry wasn't an option, even if my help was met with hostility.

Kerry's anger toward me intensified with each passing month, her rage like a misguided arrow seeking any target. I became the focus of all her pain and frustration, the scapegoat for everything wrong in her life. My attempts to reason with her, to help her see a better path, only seemed to push her further away. Each confrontation left me more drained than the last.

My own slide back into alcohol was like quicksand - so subtle at first that I didn't realize I was sinking until I was already chest-deep. Soon I was hiding bottles around the apartment, marking the levels with a pen, using all the old tricks I'd sworn I'd never return to. But even as I felt myself drowning, three lights kept burning in the darkness: Bradley's innocent laugh, Misty's tiny fingers wrapping around mine during those precious visits, and Kerry - yes, even Kerry - whose angry eyes still held echoes of my sweet little girl. They became my reason to surface for air, to keep fighting even when every breath hurt.

The shelter had taught me something crucial: I could rebuild from nothing. Each day became another small step toward healing, supported by friends who refused to let me fall. I knew now that my relationship with Kerry would need the same patient care as a damaged garden - time, attention, and endless forgiveness, not just for her but for myself as well.

Now, in the quiet moments in my small apartment, I often think about our fierce battle - a war that left no winners, only survivors. But through it all, love remained our connection, thin as a thread sometimes but never completely broken. I hold onto hope that someday, we'll find our way back to each other, both healed, both whole. Because that's what mothers do - we hope, we love, and we never stop trying, no matter how dark the night becomes.

CHAPTER 9

SETTING BOUNDARIES

Set boundaries and you won't have to build walls.
-Lenora Scurry-

For my own sanity and peace of mind, I finally had to do what felt impossible - set firm boundaries with my daughter Kerry. After years of being her financial safety net, I made the difficult decision to close the "Bank of Mom." No more help with housing payments, no more covering car insurance, no more emergency "loans" that we both knew would never be repaid. I also stopped being at her constant beck and call, available at a moment's notice whenever she needed something.

The realization hit me hard - I hadn't been helping her grow into a capable adult; I'd been enabling patterns that kept her dependent on me. While I continued providing for my grandchildren's needs - their clothes, school supplies, Christmas and birthday presents, and after-school activities - I knew I had to stop being Kerry's financial crutch, even though it broke my heart to do it.

As you might expect, Kerry didn't take any of this well. When I stopped dropping everything to collect the kids whenever she called, she began showing up unannounced at my house, dropping them off without warning and speeding away before I could object. Her treatment of me grew progressively worse, especially when I tried to maintain a loving, gentle approach. It seemed the kinder and more understanding I attempted to be, the more viciously she would lash out - screaming obscenities, calling me a worthless mother and a terrible grandmother. Deep down, I knew she was hurting, but nothing I did seemed to be enough anymore.

As her mother, feeling so completely helpless to heal her pain left me drowning in my own sense of failure and hopelessness.

In 2015, Kerry called to tell me she'd been arrested and needed me to take care of Bradley, who was five, and Misty, who was three. I drove over immediately to collect them both. Bradley should have been starting school in a week, but Kerry hadn't even registered him yet. I had to navigate a maze of bureaucracy - going before the school board and visiting Kerry in jail with a notary to get temporary custody so I could enroll him.

Taking care of the children in my small sanctuary was challenging, especially with Misty. She was still breastfeeding and missed her mother terribly. The sound of her sobbing and calling out for Kerry in the middle of the night tore at my heart.

Throughout all this, Kerry kept calling from jail, demanding money for bail. This time I held firm - she'd been arrested for failing to pay for car tags and insurance. I reminded her that she'd had the money but chose not to pay, and I wouldn't be bailing her out.

I did agree to one thing - checking on her animals at her house near Jackson Lake. When I walked in, the sight and smell nearly brought me to my knees. The house was filthy beyond description, with three or four dogs, several cats, birds, a turtle, and who knows what else. Animal waste covered the floors, and nothing had been cleaned in what looked like months. My stomach turned knowing my daughter and grandchildren had been living in these conditions.

Kerry apparently owed back rent as well, and her landlord started hounding me for the money. The whole situation was overwhelming - how could I possibly manage two small children and a house full of animals? It simply wasn't feasible. Finally, I called one of Kerry's friends who agreed to take the animals. When Kerry found out, she exploded, speaking to me like I was dirt beneath her feet. I stood my ground: "I'm not cleaning your house. I'm not helping save your stuff. I'm not taking care of all these animals. This is on you - you're an adult."

Kerry's revenge was swift. She contacted her pet group, Georgia Watchdogs, claiming I had stolen her animals. Suddenly I was bombarded with calls, texts, and Facebook messages from complete strangers. They threatened my life and called me a horrible mother, the harassment continuing until I had to temporarily deactivate my Facebook account.

As for the house itself, I never found out exactly what the landlord did with her belongings - I assume he paid someone to clean everything out. But Kerry still brings it up to this day, accusing me of stealing her animals and causing her to lose her home. I don't know what she expected me to do with a two-story house full of animal waste and junk, especially given my medical issues and having just taken custody of her two young children. I may feel like Superwoman sometimes, but even I have limits!

Eventually, as these things do, the situation passed. Once Kerry was released from jail, she got the kids back and soon began seeing another man. It seemed to me that Kerry, like myself and her maternal grandmother before her, couldn't stand to be alone - even a bad relationship was better than no relationship at all.

This new man already had a child of his own, and true to form, I welcomed both of them into my life. I treated his son as if he were my own grandchild - buying presents, babysitting, the works. But the boy had severe behavioral issues, clearly stemming from his parents' lifestyle choices. When I tried to discuss my concerns with Kerry about how his behavior might affect my grandchildren, she dismissed me entirely. "You're being overdramatic." she said. "Nothing's going to happen. Mind your own business."

That relationship didn't last long, but my relief was short-lived. Later that same year, Kerry met someone else - an alcoholic and drug user who would become Paisley's father. Despite his obvious substance abuse issues, Kerry regularly left all the children in his care. He would show up at my house drunk and high, with the kids loose in the car - no car seats in sight. The sight of my grandchildren in such danger made my blood run cold.

Every time I tried to talk to Kerry about this, she would explode in my face. I only wanted to help, but she couldn't - or wouldn't - see it that way. My worry and stress levels shot through the roof. What could I do? I knew her pain was clouding her judgment, but these were innocent children at risk.

This man, Paisley's father, is now in prison for the most unspeakable crimes that would chill you to your very soul. Every time that horrible truth crosses my mind, waves of nausea and guilt wash over me. The possibilities of what might have happened in that house - what my precious grandchildren might have witnessed or endured - haunt my darkest moments. Some nights, I still wake up in a cold sweat, wondering if I could have done more to protect them.

In my desperate attempts to shield the kids from their toxic home environment, I often had them stay with me. They would arrive with nothing - no clothes, no diapers, no formula - like little refugees from their own home. I'd rush out to buy everything they needed, my heart breaking at how normal this had become for them. Kerry would inevitably show up to collect them, demanding every single item I'd purchased. The car seats became a particular battlefield between us. I lost count of how many I bought. She would appear without any, so I'd purchase new ones to keep my grandchildren safe during their stays with me. Then she'd insist on taking them, and usually, I'd give in - the thought of those babies traveling that treacherous hour and a half home unprotected was more than I could bear.

One time, something in me finally snapped. I refused to hand over a set of car seats I'd just bought. "Go to Walmart," I told her, "Get your own, then come back for the kids." The rage that flashed across her face should have warned me what was coming. She exploded, cursing viciously, insisting she was taking mine. When I stood firm with my 'no,' she yanked open my car door and lunged for them. As I stepped between her and the seats, she began slamming the door against me repeatedly, each impact harder than the last, until self-preservation forced me to jump away. The police had to be called, and they wouldn't let her take the children until she bought proper car seats. I don't know where she found the money, but she did, and finally took the kids home. That night, I examined the bruises across my body and wondered how we'd gotten here - mother and daughter, locked in such a desperate dance.

On another occasion, Kerry appeared at my doorstep without warning, demanding I take the kids. I was barely able to stand, suffering from a brutal combination of sinusitis, bronchitis, and pneumonia. My fever was spiking, and I could hardly breathe, let alone chase after three small children. When I tried to explain this to Kerry, something in her snapped. She hurled a full water bottle at my chest with shocking force, then began ransacking my home like a woman possessed. She grabbed a garbage bag and started yanking open drawers and closets, snatching up everything I'd bought for the kids to keep at my house.

Despite all the pain and distress she caused, despite the bruises that bloomed across my chest from the water bottle, she was still my daughter. The mother of my precious grandbabies. I loved her with a fierceness that sometimes felt like it would tear me apart. We were going to figure this out together, or so I desperately believed. But the constant barrage of abuse was wearing me down to nothing.

In the summer of 2015, hoping to mend some of these fractures between us, I booked a family vacation to Panama City Beach. At first, it seemed like maybe, just maybe, this was the breakthrough we needed. The drive down was peaceful, and that first evening, watching the kids explore the hotel with wide-eyed wonder, my heart felt lighter than it had in months. These children had never seen the ocean before, never felt sand between their toes or heard seagulls calling overhead. Their excitement was contagious.

PANAMA CITY BEACH FLORIDA

Letting Go... A Mother's Journey

The next morning, I let Kerry sleep in. As a single mom to three little ones, I knew she desperately needed the rest. I got the children ready, managed breakfast, and took them to the kiddie pool just outside our room. For a few precious hours, watching them splash and play with pure joy on their faces, I could almost pretend we were a normal, happy family. Kerry joined us later, well-rested, and we actually had a wonderful afternoon together.

The day continued its peaceful rhythm - we had lunch, spent more time by the pool, and as evening approached, we all cleaned up and headed out to a local seafood restaurant. But that's when everything started to unravel. Back at the hotel, I began feeling terribly ill. Violent shaking seized my body, weakness made my limbs feel like lead, and my breathing became labored and heavy. Kerry had to call an ambulance, and I was admitted to a local hospital where I spent the next two days.

The diagnosis was diabetic ketoacidosis - a potentially fatal condition where ketones build up in the body. As I lay there connected to IVs and monitors, I couldn't help but worry about Kerry managing all three kids alone in the hotel room. After two days of treatment and a change in my diabetes medication, the hospital released me. Kerry picked me up in my car, and all I wanted was to crawl into bed with my grandbabies and rest.

Back at the hotel, I snuggled up with the kids who were watching cartoons, finding comfort in their warm little bodies pressed against mine. That's when I noticed Kerry primping - straightening her hair, applying makeup. My heart sank as I realized what was coming.

She said, "I'm going out tonight."

I couldn't believe what I was hearing. "Kerry, you can't go out - I'm still very sick," I protested, my voice weak. But she wouldn't listen.

"I had to stay here the last few days with these kids by myself. And I'm going out tonight." Her tone left no room for argument, but I tried anyway.

"First of all, you don't know anybody here - it's not safe," I pleaded. "And I'm just not physically able to take care of three children right now. I can barely move."

Her response chilled me to the bone: 'Well, you'll figure that out, won't you?' She continued getting ready, ignoring my tears and desperate pleas. At eight o'clock, she walked out the door without a backward glance, leaving me alone with three small children while I was still desperately ill.

Somehow I managed to get the kids settled and off to sleep. Then I sat there watching TV, sick with worry about Kerry. Every few minutes, I'd go to the door and look out, hoping to see her. Hours passed. She wouldn't answer her phone. For all I knew, something terrible had happened to her.

Around one in the morning, I heard a woman screaming outside. Looking out the window, I couldn't see clearly, but when I opened the door, I spotted a commotion on the beach. I recognized Kerry immediately in her bright neon orange dress. After making sure the hotel room was securely locked with the sleeping children inside, I made my way down to her.

I found her surrounded by two or three Good Samaritans who had stayed with her to keep her safe. "Ma'am," one explained gently, "we found her drunk on the beach. We didn't want anything bad to happen to her." The kindness of strangers brought tears to my eyes as I thanked them.

Getting Kerry to her feet was a struggle, but as I put my arm around her waist to steady her, something broke open inside her. She collapsed against me, sobbing like the little girl she used to be. 'Mom, I'm so sorry!' she wailed, her words slurring through her tears. "I'm such a screw-up! I'm sorry I'm such a crappy daughter! I keep trying but I mess everything up! I'm sorry, Mom, I'm so sorry!"

In that moment, all my fear and anger from the evening melted away. This was my baby girl, hurting so deeply she could only let it out when alcohol had torn down her walls. I got her back to our room and onto the bed, then lay down beside her like I used to do when she had nightmares as a child. As I wrapped her in my arms, she curled into me, still crying softly.

"I love you so much," I whispered, stroking her hair. "We're always a team, no matter what." I kept murmuring words of love and comfort until her sobs quieted and she drifted off to sleep.

In those peaceful moments before sleep claimed me too, I allowed myself to hope that this vulnerability, this raw honesty between us, might be the breakthrough we needed. But morning brought a harsh reality check. Kerry wouldn't get out of bed, and I was still terribly weak from my hospital stay.

Letting Go... A Mother's Journey

I kept trying to get Kerry to wake up, but she just cursed at me from under the covers, insisting she wasn't getting up and that I could watch the kids myself. My pleas grew more desperate as my strength waned. Finally, I gave her an ultimatum: "If you don't get out of that bed right now to help me take care of these babies, I'm just going to pack up the car and we're going home."

"Well, pack up the car and go home," she spat back.

So that's exactly what I started doing. As I packed our belongings, Kerry's anger built like a pressure cooker. Suddenly she exploded out of bed and started throwing things, yanking open the door and hurling our belongings into the parking lot by the car. Her rage was volcanic - screaming, cursing, completely out of control. I forced myself to stay calm, continuing to pack and trying to keep the children together through the chaos.

Kerry now had two choices - stay alone in Panama City or get in the truck and come home. She chose the latter, but made sure we all paid dearly for it. The entire drive home, she berated me relentlessly, her words like poison darts aimed at every vulnerable spot she knew I had. The trip became unbearable. I cried the whole way home, and so did my precious grandbabies, their little hearts breaking as they watched their mother's cruelty.

CHAPTER 10

THE OUTSIDER

Stop trying to fit in. Find the people who celebrate you for you.
-Lenora Scurry-

After that disastrous vacation, I tried to maintain some semblance of normalcy in my relationship with Kerry and the kids. But the situation with my siblings hadn't improved either. I was still consistently left out of family discussions and events, so I decided to take matters into my own hands. I began organizing what I called 'sister weekends' - I'd find nice places for us to stay and make all the arrangements and reservations myself. At first, Sheri and Melissa seemed receptive to the idea, but it wasn't long before the excuses started rolling in about why they couldn't go.

Their constant rejection was like death by a thousand cuts. Here I was, trying over and over to build bridges, to create opportunities for us to bond as sisters should, but they seemed to go out of their way to exclude me. No matter what I did, it was never enough. I found myself constantly trying to change who I was, desperately seeking their approval and love, trying to avoid their rejection. But it never worked.

I remember Melissa once telling me, "You just look for things to be offended by." My response was simple but honest: "I don't have to look for them, y'all slap me upside the head with them."

One particularly painful incident stands out in my memory. The three of us - me, Sheri, and Melissa - took a trip to Kentucky to visit Mom, who was in a nursing home by then. It was so unusual for them to include me in anything that I should have been suspicious when they asked for my help. Once we arrived at the nursing home, their true motivation became clear - they were too embarrassed to ask the difficult questions about Mom's care themselves so they chose me to be their spokesperson.

I spoke with the director about our concerns regarding Mom's care. He was very attentive, listening carefully to all our questions and complaints. He promised to prepare a detailed document addressing everything, which we could collect the next day. I felt relieved that we were finally getting some answers about Mom's situation, and that they had included me.

The next day, though, I noticed Sheri and Melissa whispering together, heads bent close in that conspiratorial way that always made my stomach churn. Sure enough, they approached me with obviously fake smiles. "We're going shopping," they announced. "We know you won't want to come because of your mobility issues." The way they said it made it clear this wasn't really about shopping at all.

My instincts were right. Later, I discovered they had gone back to the nursing home without me and collected the promised documentation about Mom's care. But that wasn't the worst part. They took those papers straight to our brother Tony's house, where the three of them sat together, reviewing everything and discussing Mom's care - deliberately excluding me once again.

To this day, I have never seen that documentation about my own mother's care. I let it go at the time, swallowing my hurt as I'd done so many times before in the name of keeping the peace. Sometimes that's what you do in families - you bite your tongue, push down the pain, and try to move forward. But there were other times when I couldn't take it anymore, when I had to speak up. Of course, whenever I did, I was immediately labeled the troublemaker, the one who always stirred things up, the one who couldn't just let things be, or as Tony used to say, "The one who wouldn't shut the fuck up."

When Mom finally passed away, I should have known that even death wouldn't bring out the best in my family. I agreed to take Kerry and the kids with me to the memorial service in Kentucky - another example of hope winning out over experience after the Panama City Beach disaster. Kerry treated the whole thing like it was some kind of all-expenses-paid vacation, with me as her personal ATM. She demanded we eat at the most expensive restaurants in town, insisted on new clothes for the occasion, and when I refused her increasingly outrageous requests, the verbal abuse would start right on cue, as predictable as a summer storm.

But Kerry's entitled behavior wasn't even the worst part. While I was in my hotel room getting ready for the service, my phone rang. It was Tony, and his opening words made my stomach clench: "I know you're going to be mad, but we're calling to let you know that Colleen is going to be speaking at Mom's memorial."

My heart dropped. Colleen was my brother Jim's wife, and she had hated me from the moment she married him - all because I maintained a friendship with his first wife. In Colleen's mind, this was some kind of ultimate betrayal, and she demanded I end that friendship. When I refused, she not only stopped speaking to me but made sure to create drama at every family gathering. The idea of her speaking at Mom's memorial was particularly galling because Mom and Colleen had actively disliked each other. I knew without a doubt that Mom wouldn't have wanted Colleen anywhere near that microphone.

I tried to express this to Tony as calmly as I could, but he immediately started raging at me. "Why can't you ever just shut your mouth?' he demanded. In the background, I could hear Sheri and Melissa chiming in with their usual refrain: 'I told you; I told you she was going to start something." They claimed they didn't want Colleen to speak either but insisted it "ain't that big of a deal.'" When I asked who had given her permission to speak, and why they were even calling me if they'd already made the decision, I was met with the familiar sound of my siblings ganging up against me. Thankfully, Colleen wound up not speaking at the memorial, which I was grateful for but once again, I was just an afterthought, the troublemaker who couldn't let things be.

By the time we got back to the hotel that evening, I was completely drained - emotionally and physically spent. But Kerry had other plans. She immediately started demanding to go out somewhere, but I firmly told her no. It was too late, I was exhausted, and besides, we were using my friend's truck for the trip, and there was no way I was letting Kerry drive it.

That's when she exploded. The tantrum that followed was epic - screaming, cursing, throwing things around the hotel room like a tornado of rage. The kids were terrified, crying and clinging to me while I begged her to calm down, to think about what she was doing to her children. But Kerry was beyond reason. I finally told her if she didn't stop, we would all pack up and go home right then and there. When she didn't back down, I started gathering our things and getting the kids down to the truck. I don't think she believed I would actually follow through, but when she saw us loading up, she finally stormed down to join us.

Looking back now, I sometimes wonder why I didn't just leave her there to find her own way home. But that's not who I am - I could never abandon my child, no matter how badly she treated me. The minute she got into that truck, the abuse began. It was Panama City Beach all over again, but worse. She called me every vile name she could think of, said she hated me, wished I was dead... at one point she even raised her fist like she was going to hit me. I genuinely worried she might try to kill me.

All I could do was keep driving and repeating through my tears, "I love you, I love you, I love you" after each cruel thing she said. But my words of love only seemed to fuel her rage. In the backseat, my precious grandbabies were sobbing, and little Bradley kept begging his mama to stop - but she was too far gone to hear even her own child's pleas.

Some time later during that awful drive, I noticed the distinct smell that meant Paisley needed a diaper change. I pulled into a gas station and told Kerry to go change her while I bought some snacks for the journey. This simple request sparked another explosion. She screamed at me to do it myself, but I stood firm and went inside the store. When I came back out, my heart sank at what I saw - Kerry was standing in the bed of the truck, throwing our belongings into the parking lot while screaming and cursing at the top of her lungs.

A crowd had gathered to watch the spectacle, and someone called the police. Only then did Kerry scramble to throw everything back in the truck and go clean up her baby. We managed to leave before the police arrived, but of course, according to Kerry, this whole scene was my fault too.

The verbal assault continued relentlessly for the remaining hours of our drive. Do you know how long it feels to listen to someone you love spewing hatred at you for hours on end? By the time we reached her house, I was emotionally raw. But Kerry wasn't done - she started violently throwing our things from the truck, repeatedly hitting the vehicle in her rage. I begged her to stop, reminding her this was someone else's truck, someone kind enough to loan it to us. Her response shocked me: "He has money, he can go buy a new one."

When I finally made it back to my haven, I was beyond exhausted. The shock of everything that had happened left me capable of nothing but crying for days. Dark thoughts crept in again, and I found myself contemplating suicide. I know now I should have made her get out of that truck and left her there, but I wasn't strong enough. I couldn't bear the thought of my grandbabies watching their grandmother abandon their mother on the side of the road.

Looking back, I sometimes wonder if that might have actually been easier on those precious children - at least they would have been spared witnessing their mother's venomous hatred toward me during that endless drive home.

CHAPTER 11

PUTTING THE KIDS FIRST ALWAYS

Courage speaks for those without a voice.
-Lenora Scurry-

2019 arrived like a storm cloud on the horizon. My baby, Kerry, now had three children by three different fathers, and she'd found herself another man - another addict, another alcoholic. I watched helplessly as he brought nothing but chaos into their lives, abusing both her and the kids. Then came the news that baby number four, my precious Harper, was on the way. My heart felt like lead in my chest, knowing the kind of world this innocent child would be born into.

The generational curse that had haunted our family was playing out again, frame by frame, like some horrible movie I couldn't stop. Night after night, I'd lie in my bed, staring at the ceiling, the same questions circling my mind like hungry vultures: How do I help her? How can I save my baby from this life? The same desperate thoughts that plagued me during her childhood now tormented me as a grandmother.

Money was always the match that lit the powder keg. They scraped by paycheck to paycheck, when there were paychecks at all. I became their safety net, their ATM, and ultimately their first and sometimes only choice. But years of experience had taught me hard lessons about enabling, and I stood my ground about not being "the bank of mom" anymore. Every time I said no, the verbal attacks would start.

Letting Go... A Mother's Journey

"What kind of fucking grandmother are you to let your grandkids be homeless?" They'd scream these words at me, each one a dagger to my heart. But I'd fire back, my voice steady even when my hands were shaking: "And what kind of parents are you to let your kids be homeless?" We all knew the truth though - those kids would never truly be without shelter. My door would always be open to them, no matter what.

My daughter's relationship with Harper's father was explosive - violence flowing both ways. I'll never forget the day Bradley called me, his young voice trembling as he told me about a fight that had ended with his mom's boyfriend being stabbed. That hour-and-a-half drive was pure torture - my knuckles white on the steering wheel, my mind spinning with horrible possibilities. What if the kids were hurt? What if things had gotten even worse after Bradley's call? Every mile marker seemed to mock me, time stretching like a big strand of salt water taffy as I pushed myself further and my car faster.

When I pulled up, the police had the boyfriend outside, blood soaking through his clothes. I burst into the house, my heart threatening to explode from my chest. The kitchen looked like something from a horror movie - blood splattered across the counter and floor. For one terrible moment, my heart nearly stopped - where were my grandbabies? Had they been hurt? Then I found them, huddled together and terrified, and my maternal instincts took over. Without a word, I gathered them up and rushed them to the safety of my car. Only after I knew they were secure did I go back to check on Kerry.

Letting Go... A Mother's Journey

When Kerry came back inside, she seemed physically unharmed but emotionally volatile. Her story tumbled out in fragments, each word laced with a mix of fear and defiance. She claimed she'd grabbed the knife in self-defense during his attack. According to her version, when he couldn't wrestle it away, he grabbed her hand - the one holding the blade - and forced it into himself.

Both Kerry and her boyfriend stuck to this story when talking to the police. But later, whispers of a darker truth started circulating - that Kerry had actually stabbed him, and he covered for her because he couldn't bear the thought of his children's mother in jail. There were six kids in that house – Kerry's four plus his two. Even now, years later, I'm not sure which version holds the truth. Kerry has always been gifted at reshaping reality to suit her needs, a trait that's both protected and destroyed her over the years.

My focus was laser-sharp on those precious grandchildren. They'd been there for the whole bloody scene - God only knows what horrors they'd witnessed. I pressed the police about interviewing the kids, checking on their welfare. They hadn't bothered - Kerry wouldn't let them in, and they didn't seem to think it mattered. When I pushed harder, they said they'd commit the boyfriend for 72 hours.

"But what about the children?" I demanded, my voice trembling with barely contained fury. The officer's response hit me like a slap: "Ma'am, what is it you expect me to do?" I reminded him about their duty to report to DFCS, watching his face carefully. He grudgingly agreed to file something, but it went nowhere - just a quick Zoom call with Kerry and case closed. No home visit, no real investigation. Nothing. Just another example of the system failing the very ones it was meant to protect.

Letting Go... A Mother's Journey

Like a bad penny, the boyfriend turned up again - these situations always follow the same tired script. Every day brought some fresh hell, too many crises to count. But there's one night that stands out, branded into my memory like a hot iron...

It was 3 AM when my phone's shrill ring cut through the darkness. Kerry's sobs came through before any words could form. When she finally caught her breath, she told me her boyfriend was beating her and she had to get out. The drive to my house was 90 minutes - too far with terrified kids in the middle of the night. She begged me to get them a hotel room, even though we both knew she didn't have a penny to her name.

It should have been simple - book a room, get them to safety. But nothing is ever simple in these situations. The hotel demanded the physical credit card at check-in. I called them, my voice growing more desperate as I tried to make them understand the urgency. After what felt like endless negotiation, they agreed to make an exception, but the process was like pulling teeth. I had to wait for faxed documents, sign everything, send copies of my driver's license and credit card, then wait for the general manager's approval. An hour and forty-five minutes of bureaucratic hell while my daughter and grandchildren sat in danger.

When they finally got cleared to check in, I was wide awake, nerves frayed raw. I called Kerry to make sure they were safe. If I'd been hoping for even a whisper of gratitude, I was fooling myself. When I asked how they were doing, she snapped, "No! What do you think?" Then immediately started demanding money for food. When I gently suggested that a thank you might be appropriate before asking for more, her response hit me like a slap: "Oh my God! You're my mother, that's what you're supposed to do!"

The entitled tone in her voice hadn't changed since she was a teenager. Nothing had changed - I was still expected to be the fixer, the ATM, the savior, and she was still as demanding and ungrateful as ever. The more things changed, the more they stayed painfully the same.

As we moved into 2020, things spiraled even further downward. Then came the moment that shook me to my very core - the moment that still haunts my nightmares - my twelve-year-old grandson threatened to kill himself. Given my own history with suicidal thoughts, this hit me like a nuclear bomb. A child that young wanting to die isn't natural. It isn't normal. Something had to change.

With a heavy heart, I hired an attorney to seek custody of the children. The decision felt like driving a knife into my own heart - betraying my daughter in the worst possible way. But watching my grandchildren's lives spiral into chaos wasn't an option anymore. They deserved stability, peace, a chance at normalcy - all the things that seemed impossible in their current situation.

Then came the night that pushed everything over the edge. Bradley called me, crying so hard I could barely make out his words. Through his sobs, I pieced together that Kerry had been screaming and cursing at him because he said he was too sick to take out the garbage. Once again, I made that familiar hour-and-a-half drive, my thoughts racing darker with every mile marker. When I finally reached them, one look at my grandson stopped me cold. His face was ghost-white, dark circles haunting his eyes, and he'd lost so much weight he looked like a shadow of himself.

Without a second thought, I got him into my car and drove straight to urgent care. The diagnosis hit like a sledgehammer - COVID. He was severely dehydrated, dizzy, and nauseous. The doctors administered antibiotics and a steroid shot, wrote prescriptions for more medication, and stressed that he needed rest and plenty of fluids.

On the drive back to his house, where I planned to pack him a bag so I could bring him home and care for him, something happened that made my blood freeze in my veins. Bradley took off his jacket, and my heart stopped. His thin arm was a canvas of horror - purple bruises like thunderclouds, angry red welts that made me want to weep, tiny cuts scattered across skin too young to bear such violence. When I asked what happened, his answer made me grip the steering wheel until my knuckles went white: "Mom beat me with an extension cord because she said I was lying about being sick."

When we arrived at the house, I confronted Kerry. My hands were shaking, not from fear but from a rage so deep it scared me. How dare she take a maternal touch and twist it into something so horrible. Hands that were designed for nurturing are now delivering calculated blows against her own child, my grandchild. But Kerry's denial came swift and cold as a harsh winter rain. "He's lying," she said, her face a mask of indifference. "I never hit him. He hurt his arm playing outside." The casual way she dismissed the evidence written across Bradley's skin only stoked the fire of my anger.

Something in me snapped. Years of watching history repeat itself, of seeing my grandchildren drowning in chaos, of trying to help someone who fought against every lifeline - it all erupted like a volcano. "I'm sick and tired of this situation," I told her, my voice trembling with emotion. "Either you change things for the better, or I'm filing for custody of these kids." Then I laid down my ultimatum: she needed to sign temporary custody of the children over to me so she could get help. "If you don't," I warned her, "I will blow your world apart."

Looking back now, I know those weren't the wisest words I could have chosen. Kerry has never handled criticism or threats well - something decades of experience should have taught me. But in that moment, my protective instincts overrode my better judgment.

Her reaction was like a bomb detonating. She exploded into a rage unlike anything I'd seen before - screaming, cursing, hurling things around the house. But what came next cut deeper than any physical violence. She turned to her children and started shouting that she hated being their mother, that they were all brats, that she wished she'd never had any of them. Even knowing it was just hurt and helplessness speaking, watching my grandchildren's faces as they heard these words from their own mother was like watching their hearts shatter in real time.

My grandbabies were terrified, clinging to me as they cried. I was crying too, but Kerry was beyond reaching. When it became clear she wouldn't calm down, I made a decision that would change everything. "We're leaving," I announced, my voice steadier than I felt, "and you're going to follow me to the bank to sign a notarized statement giving me temporary custody of these kids."

To my amazement - and honestly, my relief - she followed me to the bank. But there was a catch. She would only sign over custody of Bradley, not the girls. It wasn't everything I'd hoped for, but it was something. A start. With a mixture of relief, heartache, and happiness over the temporary custody of Bradley, I loaded up my sick grandson and his belongings, then drove him home with me. The weight of leaving the three little ones behind pressed on my chest like a boulder. Would Bradley's security mean anything if his sisters weren't there with him?

My daughter was lost and hurting, and I wanted desperately to help her, but I felt powerless. I knew these explosions of rage were her way of dealing with her own trauma and pain. This wasn't who she really was - but knowing that didn't make it any easier to watch.

Once Bradley was settled in my home, I threw myself into creating the stable life he deserved. My first priority was getting him enrolled in the local school. We went shopping together, and watching him pick out new clothes, school supplies, and his favorite shoes made my heart both soar and break. The simple joy on his face when he could choose things for himself - things that should be basic rights for any child - felt like a gift and a tragedy all at once.

Bradley had always loved golf, so I signed him up for lessons. Baseball too - anything to keep him active and engaged. I hoped these activities would give him something positive to focus on, something far removed from the chaos he'd left behind. Weekly counseling sessions were non-negotiable - the boy had been through too much trauma to just "get over it."

The transition wasn't easy. Bradley struggled with anger issues - how could he not, given everything he'd been through? Adjusting to a new school brought its own challenges. But that boy... that precious boy worked so hard. Before long, he was making the AB Honor Roll. He joined the school band and threw himself into music. When he was asked to become a school ambassador, I thought my heart would burst with pride. Despite everything life had thrown at him, despite all the pain and uncertainty, he was excelling.

Of course, I should have known that getting temporary custody of both Bradley and my granddaughters wouldn't be simple. I tried reasoning with Kerry again, explaining that this wasn't about taking her children away forever. "Use this time to get help," I pleaded with her. "I'll be here for you every step of the way. You can see the kids whenever you want." But she refused to hear it, refused to see that this was about protecting her children, not punishing her.

As I watch history repeat itself, I'm struck by the cruel irony of it all. The same patterns I fought so hard to break free from are now ensnaring my daughter and my grandchildren. The screaming matches, the violence, the constant instability - it's like watching scenes from my own past play out in technicolor. But this time, I'm on the outside looking in, and somehow that makes it even more painful.

There are nights I lie awake, remembering my own struggles as a young mother, wondering if I could have done something differently with Kerry. The truth is, even after all these years, all my therapy, all my healing - I still don't have all the answers. Maybe there are no answers. Maybe some cycles are too deeply ingrained to break in a single generation. But that doesn't mean I'll stop trying.

The space between my love for Kerry and my need to protect my grandchildren feels like an impossible chasm to bridge. Every time I reach out, she pulls further away, interpreting my help as criticism, my concern as control. Yet I can't give up on her - she's my baby, no matter how old she gets or how many mistakes she makes. I'll keep trying to find that delicate balance between tough love and understanding, between protecting my grandchildren and supporting their mother. Because that's what mothers do - we keep trying, even when it seems hopeless, even when it breaks our hearts.

CHAPTER 12

OPENING PANDORA'S BOX

*Having children is not the hard part;
learning to let them go is
-Lenora Scurry-*

During the time Bradley was with me, my attorney and I worked tirelessly for custody of all the children. Each morning, I'd wake up thinking, "Maybe today will be the day." The weight of what I was trying to do - protect not just Bradley, but all my grandchildren - felt heavy on my shoulders. I'd sit at my kitchen table, sorting through the growing stack of legal papers, wondering how things had gotten to this point.

But when Kerry was served the papers, everything changed. My own daughter - the same little girl I'd raised - went back on our agreement about Bradley staying until the end of the school year. She wanted him back immediately. Looking at her signature on our agreement now, I wondered if she'd ever meant to honor it at all.

Then came those Friday nights. Week after week, Kerry would arrive at my door with police, their patrol lights washing across my front yard. The neighbors would peek through their curtains, probably wondering what kind of trouble the quiet grandmother down the street had gotten into. My heart would race as they reviewed the same documents over and over - Kerry's signature clear as day, along with the records of abuse the children had gone through. Though she'd always leave empty-handed, the fear of those visits never went away.

During one particularly difficult visit, I could barely breathe through my panic. A female officer pulled me aside, her expression gentle. "Ma'am," she assured me, "they can't take Bradley without a court order. He's safe here with you." Those words comforted me then, though now they ring hollow. If only I'd known how temporary that safety would be.

Bradley tried to keep his spirits up through all of this. He'd still do his homework at the kitchen table, tell me about his day at school, and act like everything was normal. But I'd catch him watching out the window sometimes, especially on Fridays, looking for those police lights. No child should have to live like that, wondering when someone might come to take them away. The devastating toll it took on him started to appear as giant welts on his little body. How much more could he be pushed before he shatters?

The Monday that changed everything started like any other day. Bradley had just gotten home from school, and I was putting away some laundry when the pounding started. The sound was so violent it made the house shake - nothing like the usual police visits we'd grown used to. From the bathroom, I heard Bradley's voice, still carrying that innocent politeness that made my heart ache: "Who is it?"

When they identified themselves as police, Bradley did what we'd taught him - to be respectful to authority. But these officers wouldn't enter, not until I came to the door. Looking back, their refusal to come in should have been my first warning that this wasn't going to be like the other visits.

The hostility rolled off them in waves. Kerry had told them I'd kidnapped Bradley - a claim so absurd it would have been laughable if it hadn't been so dangerous. After all those previous visits, all those times their own fellow officers had verified my paperwork, how could they possibly believe such a thing? But the lead officer, his face set like stone, just kept repeating, "I'm here to get that boy."

"That boy," I told him, trying to keep my voice steady despite my racing heart, "has a name. It's Bradley. And you'll need a court order to take him." But he wouldn't listen. Wouldn't even look at the papers I tried to show him. Just kept saying those same words, over and over, like a broken record: "I'm here to get that boy."

What happened next plays out in my nightmares like a slow-motion film. The officer suddenly pushed past me, grabbed my arms, and before I could even process what was happening, I was face-down on my living room floor. The edge of my coffee table caught my cheek as I fell, and with my fibromyalgia, every movement felt like fire through my joints. Bradley's voice, high and frightened, cut through the chaos: "Let go of my Gammi! She has medical problems!" The officer released me in order to grab Bradley and run ou the door.

After struggling several minutes to get myself off the floor, I finally made it outside, the scene that greeted me looked like something from a crime drama. At least six police cars lined my normally quiet street, their lights painting everything in surreal flashes of blue. Kerry's truck sat in my yard, and there she was, watching it all unfold with an expression I couldn't read - my own daughter, orchestrating this nightmare.

The worst part was watching them force Bradley into her truck, his screams piercing through the chaos - begging them not to make him go, pleading for someone, anyone, to listen. My neighbors tried to intervene, especially my landlord Kathy, who'd known us for twelve years. She stood there, her voice shaking with frustration as she tried explaining everything - how the children had practically grown up at my house, about Kerry's history, about what these kids had been through. But those officers had already made up their minds. That power-drunk officer just puffed up his chest and declared, "I'm the boss now, not you." They weren't there to listen or understand - they were there to take Bradley, and nothing else mattered.

I was devastated. Throughout this whole ordeal, I'd followed every rule, jumped through every legal hoop, and kept every piece of documentation. Yet here was my daughter, telling an outright lie about kidnapping, and suddenly, all my paperwork meant nothing. Years of documented history were dismissed in an instant.

What happened next made everything even worse. The officer who'd twisted my arms and thrown me to the floor - the one who'd ignored my medical conditions - filed a false report. He claimed I'd shoved him and tried to block him from reaching Bradley. Thank God for body cameras - the footage clearly showed that never happened. But by then, the damage was done.

When my attorney finally got access to all the body cam footage, what we saw broke my heart all over again. There was Bradley, my sweet grandson, crying and begging not to go with his mom. "She beats us," he told them, his voice desperate. The officer's response? "Shut up." Even when Bradley kept trying - "You just don't know," he pleaded - they wouldn't listen. Finally, out of pure frustration, Bradley kicked at his mom's truck door. That's when this burly officer got right in my twelve-year-old grandson's face and threatened to arrest him for family violence. Can you imagine? A child crying out for help, and instead of protection, he gets threats.

This officer again lied in his report, claiming Bradley was kicking out at his mother. The body cam clearly shows her standing on the other side of the truck door where he couldn't even reach her. Just one more lie to add to the pile, one more way to make a scared child look like the problem instead of the victim.

Can you imagine what was going through Bradley's twelve-year-old mind? Here he was, being told he'd be arrested for kicking a truck door, while his mother - who'd beaten him and his sisters, left them alone for days, neglected their basic needs - faced no consequences at all. The message couldn't have been clearer: his pain didn't matter, his voice didn't count.

That officer could have chosen compassion. Could have taken a moment to really listen to a frightened boy trying desperately to tell his story. Instead, he chose intimidation, treating a child crying out for help like a common criminal. Where was the training for dealing with traumatized children? Where was the basic human decency?

I filed a temporary protective order against Kerry after she threatened me. The following Monday, a week after they'd taken Bradley, I went to court with my attorney. The Judge's first words felt like a slap: if I pursued the protective order against Kerry, I wouldn't be allowed to see my grandchildren at all. What choice did I have? I dropped it, my heart heavy with the knowledge that once again, the system was failing us.

In fact, a huge red flag was missed here because if the courts had called for his school records from the time he lived with his mom, they would have spotted that Bradley and his siblings missed more school than they ever attended, but once again all the red flags were ignored.

The Judge told Kerry to go get Bradley. What should have been a quick thirty-minute trip stretched into an hour and forty minutes. My stomach churned the whole time - I knew exactly what was happening. Kerry was coaching him, telling him what to say, what not to say. When my grandson finally walked in, he was pale as a ghost, his eyes fixed on the floor, too terrified to even look my way. My heart shattered all over again.

I think Kerry expected Bradley would be questioned right there in the courtroom where she could watch his every move, but the Judge surprised us all by taking him to his chambers for a private talk. For the first time that day, I felt a tiny spark of hope. Maybe now, away from his mother's intimidating presence, Bradley could finally tell someone the truth.

When they returned, the Judge's words to Kerry gave me whiplash: "Your life is a train wreck and yet you're sitting here saying your mother is lying. Your son has confirmed that everything his grandmother has said is actually the truth." My heart lifted for just a moment - finally, someone was hearing the truth! But then came the gut punch: "He has told me you're doing better though, so I'm going to let you keep the kids for now."

I sat there stunned. Better? After just one week? How could anyone make that judgment about the children's home life improving after such a short time, especially based on the word of a terrified twelve-year-old?

My attorney tried one last time, standing to ask, "Your Honor, Bradley is doing so well with his grandmother. Can he at least go back with her until the school year is over?" The Judge's stern "no" felt like a door slamming shut on all our hopes. Instead, he granted me visitation rights every third weekend—as if seeing my grandchildren three days a month could make up for knowing they were in danger the other twenty-six.

Through my tears, I begged the Judge to appoint a guardian ad litem - someone who could watch out for the children's interests. He refused. What was it going to take for someone, anyone, to listen? My heart shattered into a million pieces here I am pouring my soul out to the only person who can help me and he is not listening. It was as if I was frozen in time as I felt all hope seep from my body.

That's when Kerry dropped her bombshell. "She's a criminal," she announced triumphantly, "with a warrant out for her arrest." My attorney immediately objected, but Kerry produced a document - a warrant for my arrest for obstruction of an officer. This was the first either of us had heard about it. The same officer who'd thrown me to the floor had filed it the very next day after taking Bradley.

The timing made no sense. If I'd really been obstructing justice that day at my house, why hadn't they arrested me right then and there? The body cam footage told the real story - you can hear the officer saying, "This is not good, all these people are going to file complaints." They knew what they'd done was wrong, and this warrant was their way of covering themselves.

With this trumped-up charge hanging over my head, I knew I wouldn't get anywhere with the Judge. I had to let the custody issue drop, at least for now. My attorney advised me to turn myself in, and that's exactly what I did - walked into that police station to face arrest for something I hadn't done.

A "HARDENED CRIMINALS" MUG SHOT

The humiliation of that moment is something I'll never forget. Here I was, a grandmother with no criminal record, being processed like a common criminal. They took my fingerprints, my mugshot - procedures I'd only ever seen on TV shows. The holding cell they put me in held about twelve other women, some there for serious crimes. I found a corner, turned my back to everyone, and cried for nine straight hours. Nine hours of wondering how my life had come to this, how my own daughter could hate me so much that she'd rather see me in jail than let me spend time with my grandchildren.

A friend finally paid my bail, and I was allowed to go home. But those nine hours left a mark on my soul that's never quite faded. Even now, writing the words "release from jail" makes my hands shake. It feels surreal, like something that happened to someone else, except the shame and hurt are all too real.

The very next day, still reeling from the jail experience, I called DFCS again. Their response was cold and final: don't contact them again. They'd completely washed their hands of us, of four innocent children who needed help. In my desperation, I tried everything - the commissioner's office, the governor's office, the child abuse hotline, TV stations, radio stations. It was like screaming into a void. No one would listen. No one seemed to care about four children potentially in danger.

The hopelessness started to consume me like a dark tide. I'd always been the type to see a problem and immediately start working on solutions - my friends used to joke about my "superwoman mode." But this time was different. How do you fix something when every door keeps slamming in your face? The weight of it all - the trauma, the helplessness, the shame - pushed me toward thoughts of suicide again. It became a terrible balancing act, walking on eggshells, terrified that one wrong move would mean never seeing my daughter or grandchildren again. I started withdrawing from everyone, hiding away in my shame, torturing myself with endless questions: What had I done wrong? Hadn't I loved her enough? Should I have done more? I had no idea then that what was coming would be completely out of my control.

Hiding became my new normal because sharing my story felt impossible. There are these oversimplified, pervasive beliefs about parent-child relationships, especially between mothers and children. This myth of unconditional love, this idea that the bond is unbreakable. Those of us who speak about estrangement from our adult children are often judged and shamed. So I isolated myself, terrified of being ridiculed, of being labeled the worst mother of the year. After all, isn't that what I'd started believing about myself?

There was no more fight left in me. The system had won, and my grandchildren had lost. I spent so many sleepless nights crying and feeling like I had let my grandbabies down. I would pace the floor wondering and worrying what catastrophe would happen next. It was obvious that my legal efforts were of no use. What am I to do next, what next step should I take? Each day that passed with unanswered calls left me feeling more alone than ever.

The days blurred together after that, each one a hollow echo of the last. I'd wonder if I'd ever see their smiling faces again. The weight of failure pressed down on me like a physical thing - failure as a mother, failure as a grandmother, failure to protect the ones I loved most in this world. Sometimes I'd catch myself talking to their toys, explaining why I couldn't save them, begging their forgiveness for not being strong enough. The silence that answered back was deafening.

But life has a cruel way of proving that just when you think you've hit rock bottom, there's still further to fall. Like a boxer already on her knees, I was about to be dealt another blow - one that would reveal just how desperate my daughter's situation had become, and how deeply the system had failed not just me, but those four innocent children. The fight might have left me, but fate wasn't done writing our story. What came next would not only test my strength, but my very understanding of how far a mother would go to keep her children from knowing the complete truth about her.

CHAPTER 13

THE TRUTH CAN HURT – LEARNING TO LET GO

*Your wounds may run deep, but healing
lies within your own hands.
-Lenora Scurry-*

Several weeks after my time in jail, I discovered my daughter had vanished without a trace. She hadn't told anyone where she was going – not even me, her own mother. While the court-ordered visitation agreement was still in place, requiring us to meet halfway between our homes to exchange the children, it became a source of constant anxiety and pain. Kerry would show up late, if she showed up at all. Each time I waited there, my heart would race, wondering if this would be the day she'd send someone to hurt me.

Everyday my mind was overwrought with should I fight or just give up? My mind went to such dark places that I felt like I would never recover. Stone after stone, brick after brick was piling up on me to the point I didn't see a way out.

The few times she did appear, my grandchildren would climb out of her truck like little actors in a heartbreaking play. They'd put on a show of being unhappy to see me, especially little Harper, who was only three at the time. She would cry so hard she'd make herself sick, screaming and sobbing as if I were a stranger. But the moment Kerry's truck disappeared from view and we got into my car, it was like watching flowers bloom after a storm. Their faces would light up, laughter replacing tears, smiles replacing frowns. It didn't take long to realize what was happening – their mother was poisoning their innocent minds against me.

One day, while I was fixing Harper's hair in the bathroom, she suddenly blurted out something that shook me to my core. "Guess what Gammi? We're living in a shed and there are big rats." The moment those words left her mouth, she clapped both hands over it, squeezing tight, and began to sob uncontrollably.

I gathered her tiny body into my arms, settling her on my lap as she trembled. Through her tears, she choked out words that felt like daggers to my heart: "Mommy said we can't tell you anything because you are trying to take us away from her and give us to strangers."

In that moment, my world stopped spinning. The weight of what my own daughter was doing to her innocent children crushed me. How could she plant such terrible fears in their minds? I felt as though someone had reached into my chest and squeezed all the air from my lungs. A cocktail of emotions - anger, regret, confusion, worry, and shame - washed over me in waves.

The rest of that weekend was like walking through a minefield. The children seemed to measure every word, uncertain what they could or couldn't share with their Gammi. Even the simplest questions - "How's school?" or "Do you like your new house?" - would trigger Bradley into angry outbursts. "Why do you keep asking so many questions?" he'd yell, his young face twisted with anxiety that no child should have to carry.

I was walking on eggshells from that point forward; how to help my grandchildren without triggering their fear and anxiety? This ongoing uphill battle had affected my life in so many negative ways. I wasn't eating, I wasn't sleeping. I was becoming an introvert closed in by failure, guilt, and shame. This grandma's heart was shattered in so many pieces I didn't think it could ever be fixed.

Kerry eventually stopped showing up for visitations altogether, forcing me back into the familiar battleground of the courtroom. By this point, I had already spent over $50,000 - money from both my savings and generous friends - on attorneys. Now completely broke, I made what would turn out to be a devastating mistake: I went to court without legal representation.

THE COURTHOUSE IN MERIWETHER COUNTY GEORGIA

When the Judge asked about the visitations, I barely got a word out before Kerry interrupted. Then she asked to read something to the court. What followed was like watching a horror movie where you're the monster. She began reading a vicious letter she'd written, claiming I was drunk while caring for the children, that I had locked them in closets and pulled their hair. The accusations grew increasingly cruel - she said I had abused her as a child, beating her with coat hangers and abandoning her with drug addicts and alcoholics.

Anyone who knew me knew these were blatant lies. If anything, I had smothered Kerry with love and protection because of our shared trauma. The most surreal part was that her accusations perfectly described her own behavior toward her children over the years. The irony was sickening - literally. I had to excuse myself from the courtroom to vomit in the bathroom. My daughter's betrayal cut so deep I could barely breathe.

I watched in horror as her lies ripped through the room like shrapnel, each one tearing into my flesh. Who was this venomous thing who bore my daughter's face, spitting these impossible, toxic stories? She had transformed me into prey, served me up for the pack to tear apart with their judgments and hatred. The whispers and stares crushed against my chest like weight after weight, and I could feel myself sinking – not just into shame, but into a literal grave of her making, choking on each accusation as she shoveled her sophisticated lies over my broken and weary existence.

When I returned and apologized to the Judge for my reaction to her accusations, I tried to explain about the cease and desist order I'd had to file against Kerry for spreading similar lies to friends and family. I told him about her Facebook posts falsely claiming I'd kidnapped her son, stolen her car, tried to steal her identity, and how she'd posted my mugshot from the false arrest.

The Judge's response felt like another slap in the face. He looked me in the eye and sneered, "Are you done with your Jerry Springer moment?" Then he allowed Kerry to continue her tirade without ever addressing the actual reason we were there - her violation of the visitation order.

It was painfully obvious this Judge favored the mother's rights and had no interest in hearing any other perspective. My daughter took this as a green light, seeing it as having the upper hand, and from that point forward, she completely refused to let me see or even speak to my grandbabies. In desperation, I called the clerk of the court, who by now knew me quite well. I explained that my daughter wasn't following the visitation order and asked if I could file a contempt of court complaint.

The clerk paused before speaking. "Miss Scurry, may I ask you a question?"

"Of course," I replied.

"You've been to court every month for the past twelve months. The last time you were here, you were sobbing, telling the Judge you were exhausted - mentally, physically, financially, and emotionally... right?"

"Yes, ma'am."

"Okay, and has any of this done you any good?"

"No, ma'am."

"Okay," she said gently, "I would like for you to think about that."

The clerk's words hit me like a physical blow, leaving me hollow inside. After all the police reports, the documented abuse, the photos, the testimony - to be told it still wasn't enough felt like having the ground disappear beneath my feet. Every avenue I'd pursued had led to another dead end: DFCS's cursory Zoom call, the police's indifference, and now the courts themselves seeming to say "just give up." The weight of repeated failures pressed down on me until I could barely breathe. How many times can you throw yourself against a brick wall before accepting it won't move?

But here's the thing about being a mother and grandmother - you don't get the luxury of giving up, even when every logical bone in your body is screaming at you to cut your losses. So what if my savings were dwindling? So what if my health was suffering from the stress? So what if each setback felt like another piece of my soul being chipped away? When I looked at my grandchildren's faces, when I thought about the life they deserved versus the life they were living, I knew I had to keep fighting. Because sometimes the things worth fighting for are the very things that might destroy you in the process. And if that's what it took to give these kids a chance at a better life, then so be it. I'd rather go down swinging than live with the knowledge that I gave up on them. This is every mother's unwritten vow to their children and grandchildren.

Around this same time, I received a phone call from a girl I didn't know, asking if I was Kerry's mom. When I confirmed I was, she said something that I already knew, but her words still filled me with dread: "Well, I don't know if you know how they are living; the place is disgusting, full of dog feces and urine. There are no windows, and the kids have no food." Of course, I already knew about these horrendous living conditions - I'd told the Judge, shown my attorney, even presented pictures. But again, no one seemed to care.

I tried DFCS again, and as the family were now living in a different county, they were more receptive to me and instigated a visit. Although this next bit is hearsay, I believe they found the place to be unfit for habitation and gave my daughter the choice of either putting the kids into foster care, or all of them moving to live with a "productive family member". That family member should have been me, but it wasn't, it was one of my nieces.

My family may have rarely been there for me, but I do know of at least one occasion when another one of my nieces did, in fact, jump to my defense. Kerry was talking to her and told her how I never helped or supported her. My niece said, "How can you say that? She watches your kids all the time. She buys pretty much all their clothes and school supplies, provides presents at Christmas and birthdays, she goes to their school to have lunch with them, and that's only a small portion of what she does for you and your kids."

Kerry responded by saying, "well that's for them not me," my niece was flabbergasted. "How can you even allow those words to leave your mouth? If your mom never did another thing except for what she is doing now for you and your kids, that should be enough, and that is for you. Everything she does for your kids, she does for you."

As I've kept saying, with a few exceptions like the one above, my family has rarely been there for me, so of course, I didn't get one phone call from them during all this. Nobody checked on me. I sent my niece a message and asked, "Are Kerry and the kids with you?" She didn't answer, so I texted again. "My God, I'm over here dying. I'm falling apart. Can you please let me know if Kerry and the kids are at least safe?" She replied, "Yes". And I asked, "Will you tell me if the kids are in foster care?" She said, "No, they're not in foster care." And that's the last I heard from her for a while.

Being forcibly separated from those children, there were times when the "suicide monster" returned; I missed them all so much and felt so helpless. There is only so much heartbreak a mother can take. My life was spinning out of control, and my PTSD was in full swing. Everything I had been through was rushing back in, and I was totally lost and devastated.

One day, I was having an extremely emotional day and was longing for and missing the relationship I so desired with my daughter and grandchildren, so I pulled out their pictures and crawled up in my bed to go through them. I had my gun lying on the nightstand beside me, and as I sat there, it was as if this dark, monstrous thing grabbed me and was squeezing me so hard I couldn't breathe. I was gasping for air, but I couldn't catch my breath. I reached for my gun, having decided I just couldn't go on, and kept trying to put the gun to my head and pull the trigger, but something was holding me so securely that no matter how hard I tussled or tried to finagle my arms, I could not get the gun to my head. I'm not sure of the time-lapse, it seemed like an eternity, but I'm sure it was only a few minutes, then all of a sudden, this thing released me, and I sat there with the gun in my hand, thinking, "Oh my God what did I almost do?" I knew then that I had a choice to make...

This was like a nightmare I couldn't wake up from. The kind where you're trying to scream but no sound comes out, where you're running but getting nowhere. Once more, I felt utterly helpless, but the clerk's words kept echoing in my mind. After twelve months of court battles, what had I really accomplished? The truth was staring me in the face - I was destroying myself trying to save everyone else. This ongoing uphill battle had affected my life in so many negative ways. I wasn't eating, I wasn't sleeping. I was becoming an introvert closed in by failure, guilt, and shame. This grandma's heart was shattered in so many pieces I didn't think it could ever be fixed.

Taking in all the evidence, wisdom, and facts of this god awful situation, I made the hardest decision of my life: to take a step back for the sake of my own mental health. This wasn't giving up - it was survival. I had given everything I had to nurture and love my daughter and grandchildren. Through the darkest times, through the phases when she trampled over my feelings, ignored my boundaries, and drained my wallet dry. But I loved her anyway, with that fierce, unconditional love that only a mother knows.

Now that she was grown and making her own choices - choices I couldn't control no matter how much I wanted to - I had to make a choice too. I could either remain trapped in this cycle of pain and rejection she kept projecting onto me, or I could choose myself before something truly tragic happened. The gun incident had been my wake-up call. If I couldn't be there for my grandchildren because I'd destroyed myself in the process of trying to save them, what good would that do anyone?

Stepping away wasn't easy - every fiber of my being fought against it. But I forced myself to focus on healing. I started weekly counseling sessions, not just showing up but really doing the work. I began exercising, even when all I wanted to do was stay in bed underneath my cozy, comforting blanket. I did everything I could think of to improve both my physical and mental health. I wasn't sleeping more than a few hours at night, barely eating, and the depression was so deep and dark that my doctor insisted on prescribing anti-depressants. I didn't want to take them at first - it felt like admitting defeat somehow. But I knew I had to do something to help me through this dark time, so I agreed. For the first time in decades, I prioritized myself.

Then, in the middle of this recovery and recuperation period, just when I thought I was starting to find my footing again, life threw another cruel curve ball. I was sexually assaulted by my neurologist - you truly cannot make this stuff up. The bitter irony of being violated by someone who was supposed to help heal me wasn't lost on me. For legal reasons, I can't detail exactly what happened, but I did everything right: called 911 immediately, filed a complaint with the medical board, followed every proper procedure.

What I discovered next overwhelmed me with fear- this wasn't his first offense. He had been arrested for similar attacks twice before. So there I was, back in court again, this time to testify against this doctor. I thought surely, with this being his third offense, the medical board would finally revoke his license. Instead, they gave him what amounted to a slap on the wrist: take a course on boundaries and have a female chaperone present during examinations. The same exact requirements he'd been given before, which clearly hadn't stopped him from assaulting other patients. The case is still in litigation, and I'm fighting not just for myself but for every other woman who might end up in his examination room.

I remember sitting in my car after leaving the courthouse that day trying to make sense of all of this. You know that scripture that says God won't give you more than you can bear? Well, I sure wasn't feeling that truth. It felt more like I was being crushed under the weight of one tragedy after another, each new blow landing before I could recover from the last.

CHAPTER 14

LEAVING LOVE'S DOOR AJAR

*Your wounds may run deep, but healing
lies within your own hands
-Lenora Scurry-*

By this point, it had been over eight months since I'd seen or spoken to my daughter and grandchildren. The pain of their absence was like an open wound that refused to heal. In a moment of raw vulnerability, I texted my daughter, pouring out my heart. I told her how much I loved her, that whenever she was ready to get help together, I would be there. I sent simple messages just saying "I love you," hoping that maybe, just maybe, one would break through her walls. Her response knocked the breath from my lungs: "Fuck you, don't ever tell me that again." The finality of her rejection was brutal - like a door not just closing but being slammed in my face and welded shut.

Through every storm and misstep, I've held my daughter's heart in my hands, whispering 'I love you' like a prayer. Now she's taken those sacred words and twisted them into something hollow and grotesque – a mockery of everything we were. That final rejection shattered what remained of my heart, leaving nothing but echoes where love once lived.

Sometimes love means watching someone walk away, knowing your arms must stay at your sides. Sometimes it means learning to love through walls and distances, like trying to warm yourself by a far-off star.

I've learned the hardest truth now — that sometimes love means letting go.

My counselor advised me to respect her boundaries and stop reaching out, but the maternal instinct to maintain contact was overwhelming. Despite knowing it might be futile, I still occasionally send messages expressing my unconditional love and letting her know I'm here for her and the kids. Each message feels like throwing a note in a bottle into a vast ocean, hoping against hope it might somehow reach its destination.

Meanwhile, the wrongful arrest was still looming over me like a dark cloud. I had to somehow find $4,000 to hire an attorney - there was no way I'd make the mistake of appearing in court without representation again. As my new attorney negotiated with the DA, I learned they wanted me to serve ten days in jail and pay a fine. The sheer injustice of it made my blood boil.

My attorney fought back hard, pointing out the glaring problems with their case: "No way, we're not doing that he told the district attorney. The body cam footage clearly shows they were at fault. They had no court order, no documentation - absolutely nothing. And Ms. Scurry's daughter made a false report." He was fighting for me in a way the system should have been fighting for my grandchildren all along.

Finally, my attorney called with what he considered "good news." His voice was careful as he explained, "Ms. Scurry, you need to understand - this involves the police, and the DA is never going to go totally against them. What they're willing to do is have you plead guilty to disorderly conduct and pay a $350 fine."

"WHAT?" I was outraged. The very suggestion that I should plead guilty to something I hadn't done made my blood boil. "I wasn't guilty - why should I have to say I was just to save the police department's reputation?" The unfairness of it all felt like a physical weight on my chest. I looked up the legal definition of disorderly conduct: being drunk in a public place and posing a threat to others. But I had been on my own private property, stone-cold sober, and the only threat had been to my own well-being.

I told my attorney firmly, "I won't say I'm guilty when I'm not."

He sighed, clearly having anticipated this response. "Well, how about you plead 'no lo'?"

"What does that mean?" I asked, confused by the legal terminology.

"It amounts to the same thing as guilty," he explained carefully, "but I think that will just taste better coming out of your mouth."

The frustration and helplessness welled up inside me again. "I just don't see how this is right," I protested. "My daughter makes a false report, the police show up without proper documentation, they cross my threshold without permission, issue an unfounded arrest warrant, assault me, injure me, and take my grandson - and somehow I'm the one on trial?"

My attorney's voice was gentle but firm. "Ms. Scurry, I'm telling you, this is the best outcome you're going to get."

Letting Go... A Mother's Journey

The next week, I found myself back in that all-too-familiar courtroom, standing before the Judge while the district attorney spun their version of events. My attorney, who had been a beacon of support through all this, stood up and told the true story. I kept waiting for the Judge to speak up, to say "Well, if this is what truly happened, why are we even charging her?" But that moment never came. The silence in the courtroom felt deafening.

And so, with a bitter taste in my mouth and my pride in shreds, I pleaded no lo, paid the fine, and left. Walking out of that courthouse felt like swallowing broken glass - here I was, being punished for trying to protect my grandchildren. All I had ever tried to do was save them from a situation that everyone knew was wrong, yet somehow I was the one being treated like a criminal.

What makes this all even more heartbreaking is that I never even had the chance to be a regular grandmother. You know, the kind who can say to her daughter, "Bring the kids over for a couple of hours while you run errands." But that was never enough for Kerry - it was always days or weeks at a time, no middle ground, no boundaries.

I remember one particularly desperate conversation with Kerry. I asked her straight out, "What do you need from me? I feel like I'm doing and giving you everything I can." When she refused to answer, I pressed harder, "How can I help if you won't tell me what it is you think I'm doing or not doing?" I was so overwrought that I actually went to the kitchen, got a knife, and handed it to her. Through my tears, I held out my wrist and said, "Here, cut my wrist and suck all my blood dry because that is all I have left to give you."

At that point, I realized that I was just absolutely hollow inside, drained after trying everything humanly possible to create change. I had searched the darkest corners of my soul for answers, clawing through shadows for any solution I might have missed, but no matter what path I took, the ending never changed. When I finally handed her that knife, when those words left my lips – I thought surely now she would understand the depths of my desperation to help her and the children. OPEN YOUR EYES! I wanted to scream it until my throat was raw, until the words themselves could shake her awake.

That moment with the knife marked the lowest point in our relationship. As I stood there, wrist extended, tears streaming down my face, I realized something had to change. This wasn't just about Kerry anymore - it was about my own survival. The desperation I felt in that kitchen was eating me alive, consuming every part of who I was as a mother, as a woman, as a human being.

The weeks that followed blurred together in a haze of sleepless nights and tear-stained mornings. I'd find myself looking for them even when I knew they weren't there, touching their favorite toys, looking at the traces that they left behind. The silence in my house was deafening - no pitter-patter of little feet, no giggles, no calls of "Gammi!" echoing through the house.

I started seeing a counselor who helped me understand that sometimes loving someone means loving them from a distance. She taught me that boundaries aren't walls - they're fences with gates that can open when both parties are ready. But getting to that understanding wasn't easy. It meant acknowledging that I couldn't fix everything, couldn't make Kerry see reason, couldn't protect my grandchildren the way I desperately wanted to.

The hardest part was accepting that sometimes, no matter how much love you pour into someone, no matter how many sacrifices you make, no matter how much of yourself you give - it might not be enough to bridge the gap between you. That realization didn't come all at once. It came in waves, like grief, washing over me again and again until finally, I understood a fundamental truth: There is only so much of this kind of heartbreak a mother can take. I now have to live as if she is dead because I can't agree with how she is living and what she is doing to herself and her children. I miss the Kerry that I raised. I love her, and I miss her, and I want her back. Not the angry, hurting woman she's become, but my daughter - the little girl who used to crawl into my lap for comfort, the teenager who would roll her eyes at my advice but take it anyway, the young mother who once trusted me with her children.

Sometimes I find myself looking at old photographs, tracing the timeline of when things started to unravel. Was there a moment I missed, a sign I should have seen? The memories blur together - happy times mixed with the painful ones, like watercolors running into each other. I see her first steps, her high school graduation, the birth of her children... and then the gradual darkness that crept in, consuming everything we had built together.

The hardest part isn't just missing her - it's missing who she could have been. Every mother dreams of having a close relationship with her adult daughter, sharing life's joys and sorrows, watching her become a loving mother herself. Instead, I'm left with this void, this aching emptiness where that relationship should be. The what-ifs haunt me: what if I had done things differently? What if I had seen the signs earlier? What if I had found a way to reach her before the walls went up?

I hope one day, my daughter will read this and realize we are not so very different. We have both been damaged by circumstances outside of our control and have experienced terrible events, but it's what we do with those events that shapes who we become. The cycle of trauma doesn't have to continue - we can choose to break it, to heal, to become something more than our past would suggest.

She's still my daughter, and I love her with every fiber of my being. In my heart, I will never truly let her go. If she decides she wants us to seek professional help together, I'll be there in a heartbeat. My deepest prayer is that one day, she'll come to understand the depth and unconditional nature of my love for her and my grandkids. I finally reached a point where I had to accept that I had done all I could do. The serenity prayer became a big part of that acceptance because I had to let go of the things I had no control of. By doing this I then had to go through the process of feeling like I had given up on those babies.

FINDING PEACE IN SPITE OF THE STORMS

EPILOGUE

As I sit and reflect on the odyssey that has brought me to this moment, I am overwhelmed by the complexities of love, motherhood, and the process of letting go. Writing this book has been one of the hardest things I've ever done, but also one of the most healing. Each memory I've revisited and each word I've written has been a step toward understanding, forgiveness, and, most importantly, acceptance.

I titled this book Letting Go not because I've stopped loving my daughter or given up on the relationship I long for with her and my grandchildren. Far from it. My love for Kerry and her children remains steadfast, unshaken by the distance and pain. But I've learned that letting go doesn't mean letting go of love—it means letting go of control, of the guilt, shame, and toxic cycles that have kept me tethered to the past. It means allowing myself the grace to heal and to live, even as I continue to hold space in my heart for reconciliation.

For years, my life revolved around trying to fix what was broken: my relationship with my daughter, the instability in her life, and the trauma that has echoed through our family for generations. I poured all of myself into being her mother and her children's grandmother, often at the expense of my own well-being. I wanted so desperately to fill the voids in her life, to shield her and her children from the pain and mistakes I had endured. But in doing so, I lost sight of myself. I forgot that love, even the fiercest kind, cannot heal what someone else is not ready to face.

Kerry has been a central figure in my life, not just as my daughter but as a mirror reflecting the struggles, mistakes, and triumphs of my own journey. When I look back on the little girl she once was, I see so much of myself in her: the longing for love, the search for acceptance, and the resilience to keep going despite the pain. I remember her bright smile, her creativity, and her fierce independence—qualities that still shine through, even in the midst of her struggles. She is not perfect, but neither am I. She is not a villain, and I am not a saint. We are both human, shaped by circumstances beyond our control, doing the best we can with what we know.

Through documenting my own story, I've discovered that our deepest wounds often become our greatest gifts to others. Each painful memory committed to paper has become a thread connecting me to other mothers experiencing similar trauma. The stories I was most afraid to tell—the suicide attempts, the abuse, the devastating losses—have become beacons of hope for women who thought they were alone in their pain.

I've finally accepted that Kerry's pain is not solely hers to bear, nor is it solely mine to fix. It is the product of generational trauma, of a family history riddled with brokenness and survival. My mother hurt me, and I, despite my best intentions, passed down that pain to Kerry. But I also gave her love, strength, and everything I had left after surviving my own battles. And now, as her mother, I must release her to find her own path, just as I had to find mine.

Through this journey, I've been blessed with amazing friends who became the family I needed when some of my own wasn't there. Most importantly, I would like to thank my niece and nephew Erik and Denese Demonbreun, who have been my rocks, showing me what true family support looks like. When others turned away, they stood firm beside me, proving they truly are my family. Their unwavering support helped me find the courage to tell this story, to shine a light into the darkest corners of my experience.

To the readers who have walked this twisted path with me, I want you to know that you are not alone. Estrangement is a pain unlike any other, a grief that feels as though it has no end. It is the loss of not just a relationship but of hope, dreams, and the life you envisioned with your child. But even in the darkest moments, there is light. Writing this book has shown me that healing is possible, even if reconciliation is not. It has taught me that my worth as a mother is not defined by my daughter's choices, just as her worth is not defined by mine.

To my sweet grandchildren, if one day you read these words, I hope you will understand the depth of my love for you. You are my joy, my hope, and my legacy. Not a day goes by that I don't think of you, pray for you, and carry you in my heart. I hope you grow up knowing your worth, embracing your strength, and breaking free from the cycles that have held our family captive for so long. My love for you is infinite, and though I may not be with you now, I will always be here, waiting with open arms.

And to Kerry, my baby girl, my heart: I love you. I have always loved you, and I will continue to love you for as long as I live. I am sorry for the ways I failed you, for the times my own pain blinded me to yours. I am sorry for the mistakes I made, for the times I tried to control when I should have guided, and for the times I held on too tightly when I should have let go. I hope you find peace, healing, and the life you deserve. My door will always be open to you, just as my heart will always hold space for you.

Letting go is not the end of the story. It is the beginning of a new chapter, one where I choose to live fully, love deeply, and embrace the life that is still ahead of me. It is a chapter where I prioritize my own healing and happiness, not because I've stopped caring for my daughter and grandchildren, but because I've learned that I cannot pour from an empty cup. It is a chapter where I find joy in the small moments, hope in the possibilities, and strength in the lessons I've learned.

As I close this chapter of my life, I am reminded of a quote that has become a guiding light during all of this: "God, grant me the serenity to accept the things I cannot change, courage to change the things I can, and wisdom to know the difference." Acceptance has been my hardest lesson, but it has also been my most liberating. I cannot rewrite the past, nor can I dictate the decisions of others. What I can do is choose how I move forward—with grace, love, and an open heart.

If there is one message I want to leave with readers, it is this: Love fiercely, but don't lose yourself in the process. Set boundaries, not walls, and remember that letting go does not mean giving up. It means choosing to live, to heal, and to love in a way that honors both yourself and those you hold dear. It means leaving love's door ajar, always open, always welcoming, but without sacrificing your own peace.

Thank you for walking this journey with me. May my story remind you of the resilience within you and inspire you to let go of what weighs you down so that you can rise into the fullness of who you are meant to be.

With love and hope,

Lenora Scurry

APPENDIX

Here is a poem I wrote to mark my beautiful girl's first birthday:

Your First Year

Today is your first birthday. This year has gone by fast, but the memories you have given me are treasures that will last.

The laughter, the smiles, the kisses, the tears. It's all so worthwhile it's been a wonderful year.

I can't express my happiness having you as my child. Yes it's been an adventure and at times even wild.

Your shining personality has made me as proud as I can be. I hope in some small way that it is a reflection of me.

Kerry, I love you and I hope you'll always see That's God's gift to me, was you and now I'm as happy as can be.

I look at your smiling face each and every day and my heart fills with love in such a special way.

When those pretty little legs of yours took their first few steps I said thank you God, for this gift I must owe you debts.

The Lord answered to me, this child I freely give, so please love and cherish her and teach her the way to live.

I said oh blessed Lord I thank you for this soul I will love and cherish her because she has made me whole.

Kerry, Mommy loves you with all my heart can stand. Let's always be loving and each other understand.

This short first year of your blessed little world, this wonderful fun filled year I have truly adored.

I love you, Mommy.

LOVE LETTER TO MY GRANDCHILDREN

To My Sweet, Precious Grandbabies,

You all have been such a blessing to my life, and I miss you something terribly!

I'm writing this letter because right now I'm not allowed to see you.

I wish I could see you all the time. I miss our trips, parties, Christmases together, all the snuggles and kisses, your all's birthdays, and Thanksgiving. I miss every bit of it.

Bradley, you are so bright and smart and have always known what you want to do with your life, and I encourage you to stay on track and focus. I miss you being so silly and watching you create and invent. I know you're going to change the world.

Misty, you are a singer, dancer, and the best little mommy to your sisters. You have the biggest smile, and you are also very creative. I miss our talks together and the times you would become so silly, I couldn't stop laughing. I pray you find and know your worth because you deserve it all, my sweet June Bug.

Paisley, you are my sweet little horse lover who's always busy building a farm for your toy horses. You make it exact and will have a fit if someone else messes with your farm. You are my little snuggle bunny who never misses an opportunity to crawl up in my lap and ask me to sing "You Are My Sunshine." Keep that spirit, and I know you will go far!

Harper, you are my little boss diva, always trying to control everything and keeping your siblings in line. You have the sweetest laugh, and you know you are cute. You are definitely a leader, and I can't wait to see you shine.

I love and miss you all so much, but I know in my heart I will see you and be with you again. Until that time, I hope someone who reads this letter will read it to you all so you know just how much I miss having you in my life.

I want to encourage you to make the right choices and know that whatever choices you make will determine your life. Your life is what you make it.

I want you to be open and loving, but also know how to set boundaries in order to protect yourself.

I want you to know that you are worthy and that you are loved. You are strong, and you are resilient, so learn how to tackle the downs in life and use them as stepping stones and not stumbling blocks.

Wake up each day saying, "I will be the best I can be," and do it.

I know a lot has happened, and you don't understand, but when you are old enough to understand, I will tell you.

Please know that I did not abandon or walk away from you. You are being withheld from me, but I promise I am doing everything I can to get you back in my life. Sweet Dreams, my sweet babies. I love you forever.

Gammi

Here are some poems I wrote to deal with the feelings that were coursing through my veins regarding my daughter's molestation in Chapter 5: The Darkness Returns.

SHATTERED INNOCENCE

Baby is born with beautiful brown eyes and silky brown hair.

No event in the universe can even begin to compare the rush of emotions I feel.

Kisses on the forehead kisses on the cheek.

Love has blossomed between this tiny child and I.

Time passes and this beautiful infant begins to grow into a happy loving child.

She and I help each other.

We love, we laugh, we play.

My life is filled with happiness caring for her each day.

She hugs me, looks into my eyes and says Mommy I love you more than the world.

Tears come to my eyes as I look at this wondrous child I am blessed with.

So sweet, so pure, so innocent at least for a time.

Until a black heart invades this precious child of mine,

Taking away what I have tried so hard to preserve,

Shattering something that can never be replaced,

Innocence.

DESPAIR

Locked in, nowhere to turn no way out.

Feelings of despair churning all about.

My mind is jumbled, my thoughts all confused.

Feeling so helpless my energy's all used.

This monstrous anxiety creeps in and grabs me.

There's nowhere to run to, there's nowhere to flee.

I can't get up this morning. It's there holding me down.

My heart is pounding as I look all around.

The room is empty except for me and this thing.

Thought daylight was peace, a new day it would bring.

Am I crazy? Can all this madness be true?

Depression surrounds me. I'm used to it, it's nothing new.

I want to give up, take the easy way out.

I would fail at this too, I'm sure no doubt.

I'm enveloped by sadness and deep dark despair.

I can't breathe, I'm choking, I desperately need air.

Someone please help me. I'm not overreacting.

I need help.

My Sweet Baby Girl

The moment I found out I was pregnant with you was one of the most beautiful days of my life.

Even in the womb you brought me so much joy, and I planned every detail as if my life depended on it.

I was excited about every doctor's appointment and waited with bated breath for every little kick.

When you were born, oh the joy and happiness that abounded. I had NEVER experienced so many rushes of emotions as I did on that day.

And then our journey began. I loved everything about being your Mommy and was so thankful and grateful for all the joy that you brought to my life

As you grew, somewhere along the way, things began to change. I changed, you changed, both our whole lives changed and not for the better. I am so sorry that I wasn't the mother you needed or wanted. I did the very best that I knew how. Do I wish I had done things differently? Yes, but I did what I knew how to do. I gave you everything that the pain and trauma I went through didn't take away from me.

I am so proud of the woman you are becoming. I say becoming because life is a process, and we never stop growing and learning.

You have been through so much pain, and yet you keep pushing forward. I admire your tenacity and strength to keep on keeping on.

You are so talented, creative, beautiful, and smart. You are so compassionate to others and to animals, and your big, beautiful smile could light up a room.

You are brave and strong and not afraid to try new things. Your love of nature and the outdoors inspired me to start exploring it again.

I pray and believe that you and my grandbabies will be in my life again. I also pray that you find what it is you are looking for, and just know when you are ready, I'm here waiting.

I have faith in you, I believe in you, I know you can accomplish your heart's desires and make your life what you want it to be.

I am so proud of you and so thankful that you are my daughter.

I love you all the way up to Jesus and back down again.

Mom

Letting Go… A Mother's Journey

ABOUT THE AUTHOR

Lenora Scurry is a dynamic and inspiring figure, whose life's journey has been marked by resilience, self-discovery, and a deep commitment to helping others. As a seasoned life coach and motivational speaker, she uses the wisdom of her own experiences to guide women towards better relationships with themselves and others. She firmly believes in the power of self-love and setting healthy boundaries, principles that she sees as key to living a life of purpose, on purpose.

Letting Go… A Mother's Journey

With a professional background spanning over thirty-five years in advertising and marketing, Lenora has developed a unique ability to connect with people on a profound level. Her outstanding sales record and dynamic customer service skills are a testament to her dedication and expertise in her field. As the previous owner of Skyline Consulting, an advertising company, she applied these skills to create success for her clients, further demonstrating her commitment to empowering others.

Lenora's compassion extends beyond her professional life. She has volunteered at numerous women's shelters, using her expertise to bring hope and light to those in difficult circumstances. Her work at Teen Challenge, where she worked closely with residents and their children, is a shining example of her dedication to making a difference.

In her debut book, "Letting Go… A Mother's Journey", Lenora shares her deeply personal story of love, loss, and heartache. The book captures her experiences from her childhood to the present, detailing her complicated relationship with her estranged family and daughter, and her deep bond with her four grandchildren. Despite the obstacles and unimaginable emotions she has faced, Lenora's narrative is a powerful story of survival and hope.

"Letting Go… A Mother's Journey" is not just a recounting of struggles, but a celebration of overcoming adversity and finding inner strength. Through her book, Lenora hopes to inspire others to find their own path to resilience and self-love.

www.ingramcontent.com/pod-product-compliance
Lightning Source LLC
Chambersburg PA
CBHW070948180426
43194CB00041B/1746